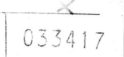

Computers
and
Common Sense

Fourth edition

ROGER HUNT
JOHN SHELLEY
Imperial College, London

PRENTICE HALL
New York   London   Toronto   Sydney   Tokyo

First published 1988 by
Prentice Hall International (UK) Ltd,
66 Wood Lane End, Hemel Hempstead,
Hertfordshire, HP2 4RG
A division of
Simon & Schuster International Group

© **1988 Prentice Hall International (UK) Ltd**

Printed and bound in Great Britain by
A. Wheaton & Co. Ltd, Exeter

Library of Congress Cataloging-in-Publication Data

Hunt, Roger, 1936–
   Computers and commonsense.

   Bibliography: p.
   Includes index.
   1. Computers.   2. Electronic data processing.
I. Shelley, John.   II. Title.
QA76.H797   1988   004   87-7244
ISBN 0-13-162744-9 (pbk)

British Library Cataloguing in Publication Data

Hunt, Roger, *1936-*
   Computers and commonsense. – 4th ed.
   1. Electronic digital computers
   I. Title   II. Shelley, John, *1940-*
   004   QA76.5

   ISBN 0-13-162744-9

---

2 3 4 5   92 91 90 89

ISBN 0-13-162744-9

a year. Fingerprint identification, in time to catch a criminal before he flees the country, would be impossible without computers. The first example enables us to enjoy knowledge that would otherwise be unobtainable within our own lifetime. In the second example, the police gain time in which to act.

Storage The speed with which computers can process large quantities of information has led to the generation of new information on a vast scale, in other words, the computer has compounded the information explosion. How can people cope with it? We can't, but computers can. But where do they keep it all?

As a human acquires new knowledge, the brain subconsciously selects what it feels to be important and worth retaining in its memory, and relegates unimportant details to the back of the mind or just forgets them. In computers, the internal memory of the CPU is only large enough to retain a certain amount of information (i.e., it is *finite*). It is, therefore, impossible to store inside the computer the records, for example, of every Premium Bond and the names and addresses of their owners. All of this data is stored outside the memory of the CPU, on *auxiliary* or *secondary* storage devices, usually magnetic tape or disk (see Chapter Four). Small sections of the total data can be accessed (got at) very quickly by the CPU and brought into the main, internal memory, as and when required for processing.

The internal memory (in the CPU) is built up in 1K or K modules, where **K** equals 1024 storage locations. Babbage's Analytical Engine would have been capable of holding 1000 numbers, each of 50 digits. Computers come in many sizes. Many small microcomputers have an 8K or 16K store whilst 'super computers', such as the CDC CYBER 205 may have up to 1024K stores (i.e., 1024 x 1024 locations).

Accuracy In spite of misleading newspaper headlines (*Computer demands account for £0.0 to be settled immediately*), the accuracy of computers is consistently high. Errors in the machinery can occur but, due to increased efficiency in error-detecting techniques, these seldom lead to false results. Almost without exception, the errors in computing are due to human rather than to technological weaknesses, i.e., to imprecise thinking by the programmer, or to inaccurate data, or to poorly designed systems. The design of computer systems is discussed in detail in Chapters Seven, Eight and Twelve.

Versatility Computers seem capable of performing almost any task, provided that the task can be reduced to a series of logical steps. For example, a task such as preparing a payroll or controlling the flow of traffic can be broken down into a logical sequence of operations, whereas comparing the tones of a Turner with a Vermeer cannot. Yet

Contents

Preface
to the fourth edition

The first edition of this text, in 1975, was conceived and written in order to provide a general guide to basic computing concepts for a growing population who found it necessary to come to terms with the computer. Since that time, computer technology has made enormous strides. It is still marching forward promising even more wonderful advancements within the next two decades. The microcomputer is the latest of the current developments. But apart from its technology it has had a far reaching impact upon society as a whole. Who today in industrial societies has not heard of the microchip? Who tomorrow will not be faced with microelectronics at work, in the home and within society at large? Yet the basic concepts remain the same. This fourth edition is as relevant today for those seeking an entrée into the world of computers as the first was for those in 1975.

We would like to thank our editors at Prentice Hall for their enthusiasm in encouraging this latest revision and for providing us with the opportunity to incorporate many of the more recent technological developments.

R.H.
J.S.

Introduction

'Computing' is now an everyday term in our language. Computers are referred to in the press, on the radio and TV, and they appear in films and books – with and without an aura of science fiction. But what do they mean to you? Some people may be exhilarated at the prospect of a computerized society, others may be despondent; some may be sceptical, and many may be cheerfully indifferent to the whole subject. These attitudes apply to any topic which seems specialized and about which we know little, and which thereby acquires a certain mystique. We may know little, for example, about medicine or the law, but these are older disciplines and methods have been evolved (generally known or easily available to those who need them) by which we can find the right person to give us the right advice. Now, however, computers are ubiquitous and, for all their apparent complexity, they seem to have a wide range of uses and play an ever-increasing role within our society. So, where does one find out about them?

It is the aim of this book to remove the mystique that may surround the subject. We shall do so by trying to answer three basic questions: *What is a computer? What can it do? How can one communicate with it?* The outline given in this book will not make you an expert but, we hope, will provide sufficient background on the fundamental principles to enable you to think sensibly and talk intelligently about computing, and to show you where more specialized information, should you need it, can be found. You should be able to see the fallacies in such headlines as 'Computer makes firm bankrupt', and 'Computer kills 80-year-old woman' and be able to think through what might have happened, how, and by whom. We hope that you will be able, when watching films and TV, to see through the technical charade of whirring tapes and winking lights so that you can better evaluate that which is probable and that which is fanciful. If this book provides the means whereby you can, in Darwinian terms, 'survive', that is *successfully* adapt to the computerized society, then we shall have achieved our objective.

We aim to answer the following questions:

1 *What is a computer?* This entails a definition of computing as well as a discussion about the basic anatomy of computers, their powers and limitations. This leads on to the present-day situation in which computers are often 'hidden' from the general

user within computer 'systems' and their operating 'software'. Chapters 1, 2, 3, 7, 8 and 12 are related to this first concept.

2 *What can they do?* We consider the uses and/or applications of computers. Various issues raised by present and possible future applications are discussed. Related to this second concept are chapters 9, 10, 11 and 13.

3 *How does man communicate with computers?* This covers two broad aspects. Because of structural differences (the neurological mismatch) between man and machines, we need to 'communicate' with machines via special, though restricted, 'languages'. What programming languages are, and how they are used to instruct machines, is introduced in chapters 5 and 6. The second aspect is that of the input–output devices, those parts of the machine which convert information from the real world of man into formats which can be handled by computers. Chapter 4 covers this aspect.

The text contains the essential material relevant to these three concepts. As the *applications* of the concepts increase in sophistication, it sometimes becomes necessary to stop and develop a particular topic so that its relationship to other, subsequent, elements can be appreciated. The sequence of chapters takes this into account and the logic of the structure of the book will become more apparent as you work through it. Additional background information and technical details are included in the appendices. We have tried to eliminate jargon as much as possible. Definitions are given where necessary and a Glossary and List of Acronyms are included at the end of the book, together with a Bibliography of further readings and an index.

of gears and wheels, for transferring data between the mill and the store

- and *input device* to pass into the machine both numbers (the data) and instructions as to which of the arithmetical operations to perform
- an *output device* to display the results obtained from the calculations.

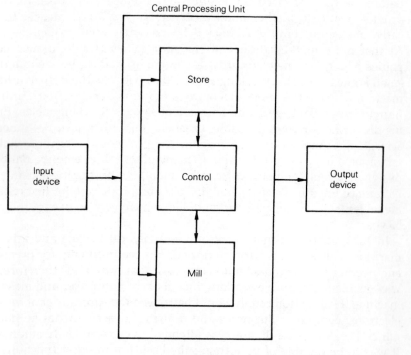

Figure 1.1

Figure 1.1 shows these five parts in an arrangement which closely resembles the basic anatomy of today's computer. The three parts consisting of the Store, Mill and Control units are collectively known, in current terminology, as the Central Processing Unit (CPU) (discussed in greater detail in the next chapter). It is this to which we really refer when talking about the computer. The other two units, the Input and Output devices (I/O) (see Chapter Four), are concerned with entering information (instructions and data) into the CPU, and with outputting the results once processing has taken place.

1

An Introduction to Computing

WHY WAS THE COMPUTER INVENTED?

Many of the routine activities in today's society are performed by computers. For example, when we go on holiday our 'plane seats are often reserved by computers; the traffic in some major cities is, to a degree, controlled by computers; the egg which you might have had for breakfast may have been laid (no, not by a computer!) by a chicken whose life history is on record on a computer file; many of the bills we pay (rates, gas, electricity, telephone, insurance, etc.) are calculated and printed by a computer. Why? And how?

It was outlined in the Introduction that there are three essential concepts that we need to examine in order to be able to think sensibly and talk intelligently about computing – What are computers? What can they do? How can we communicate with them? But first of all, what do the terms *computer* and *computing* mean?

Obviously computing has something to do with reckoning or calculation, but man has been using his brain to do just that for centuries. The Egyptians built the pyramids; whoever built Stonehenge left a calendar which can still accurately predict eclipses; the Romans designed and built long straight roads, aqueducts and heating systems; early explorers navigated the globe, and even radio and television were invented – all without computers. What is so special about them that we need computers today? It cannot simply be because they are calculating devices. We have many forms of such devices – the abacus (still used in the Far East), pocket and desk calculators, even supermarket check-out tills – all of which are cheaper and easier to use than computers. So, why was the computer invented?

Because it had to be! The pressures of World War II dictated research in many areas. The new use of night bombers, submarines, and long range guns on ships and tanks meant that armies had to fight by shooting at targets they could not see. Technology, in the form of radar, was developed to locate the enemy: where he was, in which direction he was moving and how fast he was travelling. It was then necessary to aim guns so that when the shell was fired it would reach the enemy at the point to which he had moved. This could not be done with any accuracy without first performing detailed mathematical calculations. Firing tables were required by the men at the front line so that the figures were immediately available. But these figures were not in existence because the human effort involved in producing them was too great. What was needed was a machine which could produce the tables with the required speed and accuracy. Huge sums of money and brainpower were combined to produce the technology. In 1942, the Ballistic Research Laboratory of the US Army Ordnance Department began work with the Moore School of Electrical Engineering. As a result, a computer named ENIAC had a formal dedication ceremony on 15 February, 1946 (see Appendix One). ENIAC was able to produce the tables by carrying out the huge number of calculations involved, accurately and to the required precision and, because it was electronic, at a speed which made it all possible.

The problems which early computers had to solve were mostly mathematical. Today, computers are used to forecast the weather, to operate machines to cut shapes out of sheet metal, and even to guide spacecraft to the moon. They can set and print newspapers and books. They can be used to help in diagnosing diseases and to find out whether a hospital bed is available for a particular patient. They are used to find obscure documents in archives and elusive criminals on the run. Travel agents around the world have come to rely on them to book seats on air flights or rooms in hotels, either today or a year from now. Companies use them for accounting, invoicing, stock control and payrolls. Computer **applications** are discussed in detail in Chapter Nine.

The original objective for inventing the computer was to create a fast calculating machine. But in over 80% of computing today, the applications are of a non-mathematical or non-numerical nature. To define a computer merely as a calculating device is to ignore over 80% of its work, rather like someone refusing to believe that the bulk of the iceberg lies hidden under the water. If not as a calculating device, then how are we to define a computer?

If we return to the brief list of applications above, we can discern one key fact: computers act upon information. This information or **data,** comes in all shapes and sizes, from a mathematical equation to the required details about a company's work-force necessary to produce a payroll, or to the myriad of data needed to project an Apollo craft

through space. The fact that computers process information fundamental, some experts have coined a word for it – *informatic* science of information processing, i.e., the methods of recor manipulating and retrieving information. Many people believe this the essence of computing.

THE MACHINE

Before the days of electrical engineering, attempts had been ma provide results to mathematical problems by *mechanical* means. early nineteenth century, Charles Babbage came closest to succee At that time, mathematical and statistical tables (for insurance panies and government records, for example) had to be compil small armies of clerks. Working as they did, without the help of a machines, even the most elaborate precautions could not elim human errors. Babbage spent many tedious hours checking tables. his dissatisfaction and, probably, exasperation with the clerks' in acies, came the idea of a machine which could compute guaranteed to be error-free. Among many other achievements, Ba designed several 'engines' as he called them, the first of these bei Difference Engine. This was built in 1822 and produced the first re life tables (statistics of expectation of life) which were in use for th 50 years.

In 1833, Babbage began work on his Analytical Engine and it i machine with which we are concerned. His requirements for pre engineering were impossible to achieve at that time and, therefor was unable to produce a working model of the complete, and ma machine. Had he done so, it would have been the forerunner of to electronic computer. But notes and drawings describe what he h mind. The Analytical Engine was intended to be completely autor It was to be capable of performing the basic arithmetical function *any* mathematical problem and it was to do so at a speed of 60 add a minute. The machine was to consist of five parts:

- a *store* in which to hold numbers, i.e., those which we provide the information (data) for the problems, and those v were to be generated during the course of calculations
- an *arithmetic unit* which Babbage called the 'mill'. This was to device for performing the arithmetical operations on the nun which had been stored. All the operations were to have carried out automatically through rotations of gears and whe
- a *control unit* for seeing that the machine performed the de operations in the correct sequence and, also by means of a

Information in the computer

Whereas the Analytical Engine of Charles Babbage was to have been mechanical, today's computers are electronic. We do not define the term electronic in this book, but its use in defining the computer as an electronic calculating machine implies a machine in which all information is indicated by one of two states; either an electrical pulse is present or it is absent. For an electronic computer to be able to store our everyday, written characters, it has to be able to identify them as patterns of electrical pulses (see Chapter Two). For the moment, try to visualize a sort of morse code where the dashes and dots are replaced by the presence or absence of an electrical charge. If the presence is indicated by 1 and the absence by 0 (zero), and, if the pattern 000 means S and the pattern 111 means O, the distress signal SOS (... --- ...) would then appear as 000 111 000.

The 1's and 0's are known as **binary digits,** or **bits.** The number of symbols that can be coded into bits will depend upon the number of binary digits that one allows for each symbol. If one were to allow 6 bits per symbol, one could encode up to 64 different symbols because six bits can be arranged in 64 unique ways (see Figure 2.2). It doesn't matter if you do not understand why at this particular point, provided that you can accept that the more bits you have, then the more different symbols you can encode. You should be able to appreciate that with 64 patterns, it is possible to encode not only the 26 letters of the alphabet and the 10 decimal digits, but also up to 28 special symbols to include punctuation marks, mathematical and monetary signs.

We have said that the essential point about computers is that they process information, and we have looked, briefly, at how information is represented in the computer. Our task, now, is to consider the nature of this information. As human beings, we continuously make value judgements about the information we receive and instinctively process. A particular piece of art, whether a painting, piece of music or whatever, will attract some people but it may bore or even repel others. Our judgement of it will be based on our feelings, taste, knowledge and experience. But computers cannot make such judgements. They are devoid of emotions. A computer can be programmed (instructed) to generate poetry or music, but it cannot appraise it or judge its quality. Computers have no 'feelings' and no 'instincts'. They are machines and whilst one can build into them the equivalent of a 'memory', one cannot build into them the equivalent of a 'heart' and 'soul'. The human brain subconsciously acquires certain priorities (in the sense of making choices or determining selections based on experience, taste and individual needs). A computer cannot. It has to be consciously programmed to follow our chosen priorities. Computers can help mankind but they do not threaten it. They are only as good as man makes and uses them.

Computers approach their information in a restricted or logical manner. (This is discussed in greater detail in Chapters Five and Six.) If a task is capable of being reduced to a series of simple (individual) logical operations, then it can be performed by a computer, much more quickly than humans could do it. Much of the work currently carried out by humans is of a logical nature and it is this which accounts for the ever growing list of computer applications rather than, as some may imagine, the 'power-lust' of the computer itself. If, for example, you analyse what is involved in driving an underground train or in assembly-line work, you will find that much of it is essentially logical (i.e., series of sequential, separate steps). Programmers, the people who are responsible for instructing computers, are therefore required to demonstrate *logical* rather than *mathematical* abilities. To grasp the point that the computer is a logical machine is to help put computers in their correct perspective and to show more clearly those areas where the computer is *not* in competition with man. This is covered in Chapter Thirteen.

Finally, it is important to appreciate that once a computer has been given a piece of information, it is capable of remembering it at any time. In this sense, it is far superior to a human being. Although we assimilate much information during our daily lives, we sometimes have difficulty in remembering particular things (names, places, dates, etc.) just when we need them. The computer, however, can always access (find) any piece of information that it has in store, and this data can be reproduced tomorrow, or in years to come, exactly in its original form – providing that nobody has deliberately changed it.

Input/output devices

The function of **I/O devices** is to get information into, and out of, the CPU. We could use binary digits and make a device which would send an electrical pulse through the memory unit when it sensed a 1 bit, and not send a pulse when it did not sense a 1 bit (i.e., binary 0). Some of the first programmers did just that. The input device was then a very simple machine, but it made life very difficult for the programmer because it is not always easy to think only in terms of 1s and 0s. Developments soon led to more complex devices which can translate into binary patterns those characters and symbols which are familiar to us in everyday life.

A company preparing its payroll will have certain information about each worker, e.g., his name, number, department, gross pay, tax concessions, etc.

BILL BROWN, 007, GENERAL OFFICE DEPT., GROSS PAY £XXX, TAX £YYY . . .

Each of the above characters – the letters of the alphabet, the numbers, full stop, comma and the £ symbol – can only be represented in the CPU by unique (individual) binary patterns. If Bill Brown were to get his pay slip in binary he would not be able to read it. The output from the computer must, therefore, also be in a *human* readable form. The input devices translate the characters into binary, and the output devices *re*translate them back into the familiar characters that Bill Brown can recognize. The purpose of the I/O devices is to act as translating devices between our external world and the internal world of the CPU, i.e., they act as an **interface** between humans and the machine.

CHARACTERISTICS OF COMPUTERS

Speed   The computer was first conceived as a high-speed calculator. This has led to many scientific projects being carried out which were previously impossible. The control of the moon landing would not have been feasible without computers, and neither would today's more scientific approach to weather prediction. If we want tomorrow's forecast today (and not in six months' time) meteorologists can use the computer to perform quickly the necessary calculations and analyses. When making flight reservations we want to know well in advance of take-off that a seat will be available – if it is not, then we need to have time to make other arrangements. The ability to get answers fast enough so that one has time to take action on them (or to make alternative plans, as in the case of airline reservations) makes **real-time computing** possible and this is discussed in Chapter Seven.

Electrical pulses travel at incredible speeds and, because the computer is electronic (and not tied down to mechanical movements, turning of wheels, slipping of clutches and gears), its internal speed is virtually instantaneous. We do not talk in terms of seconds or even, today, of milliseconds (thousandths of a second). Our units of speed are the microsecond (millionths), the nanosecond (thousand-millionths) and even the picosecond (million-millionths). A powerful computer is capable of adding together two 18–digit numbers in 300 to 400 nanoseconds (i.e., about 3 million calculations per second).

Consider two examples from non-numerical environments. The manual indexing of the complete works of Thomas Aquinas (approximately 13 million words) would have taken 50 scholars about 40 years to accomplish. With the aid of a computer, a few scholars did it in less than the computer itself has only limited ability and, in the final analysis, actually performs only *four* basic operations:

- it exchanges information with the outside world via I/O devices;
- it transfers data internally within the CPU;
- it performs the basic arithmetical operations;
- it performs operations of comparison.

In one sense, then, the computer is not versatile because it is limited to four basic functions. Yet, because so many daily activities can be reduced to an interplay between these functions, it appears that computers are highly ingenious. Programming is the craft of reducing a given problem into an interplay between these few operations (see Chapters Five and Six).

Automation A computer is much more than an adding machine, calculator or check-out till, all of which require human operators to press the necessary keys for the operations to be performed. Once a program is in the computer's memory, the individual instructions are then transferred, one after the other, to the control unit for execution. The CPU follows these instructions ('do this', 'do that', 'do the other', etc.) until it meets a last instruction which says 'stop program execution'. When Babbage claimed that his Analytical Engine would be *automatic*, he meant that once the process had begun, it would continue without the need for human intervention until completion.

Diligence Being a machine, a computer does not suffer from the human traits of tiredness and lack of concentration. If 3 million calculations have to be performed, it will perform the 3 millionth with *exactly* the same accuracy and speed as the first. This factor may cause those whose jobs are highly repetitive to regard the computer as a threat. But to those who rely on a continuous standard of output, e.g., quality control in the refining of oil and other chemical processes, the computer will be seen as a considerable help.

We began by pointing out some of the uses of computers. We conclude this chapter with a quotation that aptly underlines their significance:

Yesterday people questioned our ability to build a **digital** computer. Today the computer has already shown that it is one of man's great tools, and that its potential benefits for mankind are tremendous. But these benefits are not inevitable; nor are they unmitigated. We will have to work hard to realize the benefits fully. The entire world will have to plan carefully to avoid the dangers that accompany progress.

It is important for us to remember – and for the rest of the world to realize – that the computer has begun an information revolution that will profoundly affect the lives of everyone. I realize that these are strong words.

Not everyone will agree that the changes in progress are actually revolutionary. But the computer and modern information processing techniques do far more than amplify man's physical force, which was the basis of the industrial revolution. These tools amplify man's ability to manipulate information. This amplification will cause revisions in our economic, government, and social structures as drastic as the ones caused by the industrial revolution.

(Auerbach, *see* References)

We have looked at the meaning of computing, analysed the basic structure of the computer, and discussed its characteristics. We shall now extend our examination more deeply as follows:

Chapter Two   looks at the basic anatomy and structure in more detail;

Chapter Three   discusses the basic anatomy of the microcomputer in relation to the structure of the traditional computer;

Chapter Four   investigates the various I/O devices which interface between the CPU and the real world of man, and considers auxiliary storage media;

Chapters Five and Six   discuss programming, and modes of communication between men and computers (computer 'languages');

Chapters Seven and Eight   expand our view of the basic machine to consider it more properly as, and within, a computer *system;*

Chapter Nine   looks at some of the many uses to which computers are applied;

Chapters Ten and Eleven   investigate the concepts of information *structuring* and the preparations necessary for computer processing of data;

Chapter Twelve   outlines the organization and personnel required to operate a computer installation;

Chapter Thirteen   discusses the implications for society of the computer.

2

The Basic Anatomy of the Computer

A reference has been made to a **digital** computer. By inference, the digital machine is one which operates essentially by counting (using information, including letters and other symbols, in coded form represented by two-state electronic components). This is in contrast to the analog computer which operates by measuring rather than by counting. The analog machine, because it has only a limited memory facility and is restricted in the type of calculations it can perform, can only be used for certain specialized engineering and scientific applications. Most computers are digital. Indeed, the word 'computer' is generally accepted as being synonymous with the term 'digital computer'.

BASIC STRUCTURE

Remembering Babbage's Analytical Engine, let us see what happens in a computer. It receives information (input); it processes this information in some way according to a set of precise instructions (in the CPU); and it then presents the results in a useful form (output).

On closer inspection we find that the CPU (the computer itself, remember) has to store the information in a memory before it can carry out any processing operations. Two kinds of information have to be input, the program and the data. The program is the set of instructions which the computer is to carry out, and the data is the information on which these instructions are to operate. For example, if the task is to sort a list of telephone subscribers into alphabetical order, the sequence of instructions or procedure which guides the computer through this operation is the program, whilst the list of names to be sorted is the data.

11

In the Analytical Engine calculations were to be handled by an arithmetic unit which Babbage called the mill. The computer also has an arithmetic unit. Arithmetic, because *all* computer operations involve the manipulation of numbers. All information, programs and data, are represented in numeric form (bit patterns). The manipulations also include making comparisons and logic type operations as well as arithmetical operations (+ − × ÷), and for this reason the unit is referred to in full as the Arithmetic and Logic Unit (ALU). The significance of comparisons and logic-type operations is discussed further in Chapter Six.

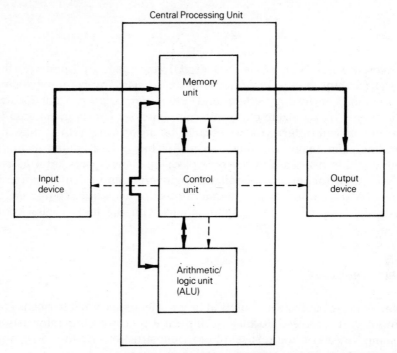

Figure 2.1 Basic structure of the computer. In the case of the microcompu-
ter, the structure is depicted differently (see Chapter Three).
However, the concept of operation remains the same; it is merely
that the technology enables the various functions to be organized
in a different way

In order to ensure that information is correctly placed in store, and that the program instructions are followed in the proper sequence and data is selected from memory as necessary, a control unit is required.

The control unit, together with the ALU and memory unit, form the Central Processing Unit (CPU). Figure 2.1 differs from figure 1.1 only in that the mill has now become the ALU and the word 'memory' has been used instead of 'store' (the two being synonymous). However, with the different use of arrows we can indicate the flow of information (full lines) and the control of events (dotted lines), and extend our appreciation of the significance and role of the control unit.

The program instructions and data are transferred, **under the direction of the control unit,** from the input device into the memory. During program execution, each instruction is retrieved in turn (proper sequence) from the memory and interpreted. Control informs the ALU of the precise operation to be performed and directs the transfer to the ALU of any item of data which is needed for the operation. The ALU then executes all calculations and comparisons. Results destined for output are then passed to memory where they are held in storage temporarily, prior to presentation by the output device. This procedure also takes place under the direction of the control unit.

A CLERICAL EXERCISE

How does a human being handle a particular problem? Suppose you are asked to determine the number of candidates who have passed a certain examination and to make out a list, or lists, of their names.

First of all you need the lists of candidates who took the exam, together with the marks that each obtained. This is your *data*.

You need to know what the pass mark is, and guidelines as to how the final lists are to be presented, i.e., alphabetically by names, or numerically from the highest mark to the lowest, or both. You can then devise a plan of how to process the information to achieve the desired result(s). This will be your program. You will commit some of your plan to memory and you may need to jot down other parts of it to remind you as you work through the problem. The computer, however, has to be given the *entire* plan or program which is then stored in its memory unit.

Are you allowed to write on the exam papers themselves? If you are, then you could put a √ for a pass, and an X for a fail on each paper. You could then separate the papers with ticks and count them up. You could also sort them alphabetically and/or in mark order as necessary, and from your sortings you could make out the desired lists. If you are not allowed to write on the papers, you could sort them one way first, say alphabetically, and then make out that list. You would then have to re-sort again, say numerically, and make out another list. Alternatively, you could make out rough lists in random order as you went through the papers. You could then number your results in the desired sequences, perhaps using different colours, say red for the alphabetical sequence and green for the numerical sequence. You would then be able to make out two final lists from the one, rough, marked list. Yet another method might be to list the results on separate pieces of paper or index cards, sort the cards one way and make out a list, re-sort them another way and make out a different list. The method that you choose might seem to be a matter of personal preference. In fact, it will be determined by the information that you are expected to produce (the number of lists and the complexity of the information the lists are to contain); what you are allowed to do with the data (could you photocopy it and then mark the photocopies?); and the materials, including *time*, which may be available to you.

Suppose you need to compare the number who passed with the number who failed; or the range of marks (highest to lowest) of all the candidates, or only of those who passed, or only of those who failed; or the average mark; or how many were above this average and how many below it. You need to know what is required now, and what may be needed later, before you can devise the best way to proceed, in a series of strictly logical and separate steps.

Try to think of ways in which you can gather as much information as possible during one detailed check through the papers, and of how this information can be sorted in the several ways you need, without having to recheck through the papers again and again. This is what a programmer would have to do in seeking a computer solution to the problem.

DATA REPRESENTATION WITHIN THE COMPUTER

Information is handled in the computer by electrical components such as **transistors, integrated circuits, semiconductors,** and wires, all of which can only indicate two states or conditions. Transistors are either conducting or non-conducting; magnetic materials are either magnetized or non-magnetized in one direction or in the opposite direction; a pulse or voltage is present or not present. All information is represented within the computer by the presence or absence of these various signals. The binary number system, which has only two digits, zero (0) and one (1), is conveniently used to express the two possible states.

All the familiar symbols which we use in *written* information are represented in the computer by combinations of bits (a unique pattern for each symbol). A 'set' of such combinations of bits would include the letters of the alphabet, the digits 0–9, and certain special characters such as punctuation marks. A set containing all these characters is known as an '**alphanumeric**' (or alphameric) **character set.** For example, let us use a combination of six bits for each character. Since six bits can be arranged in 64 different ways, this allows for a 64–character set (see figure 2.2). Five bits per symbol would only provide 32 possible permutations and this would be totally insufficient for the number of characters we need to represent. In reality, six bits with 64 permutations is also insufficient when you consider the need to distinguish between upper and lower case letters. Thus, 8 bits which gives 256 unique permutations is common, which allows not just for numbers, letters and punctuation but for scientific symbols as well.

Computer words

We express information in **words.** So do many computers. A computer 'word' is a group of bits, the length of which varies from machine to machine, but it is normally predetermined for each machine. The word may be as long as 64 bits or as short as 8 bits. In many computers the fundamental grouping of bits is called a **byte** rather than a word. A byte is usually shorter than a word, typically consisting of eight bits. An eight-bit byte can, for example, be used to represent one alphanumeric

Decimal number	The binary equiva-lent represented by six bits	Character repre-sented		Decimal number	The binary equiva-lent represented by six bits	Character repre-sented
0	0 0 0 0 0 0	none		32	1 0 0 0 0 0	5
1	0 0 0 0 0 1	A		33	1 0 0 0 0 1	6
2	0 0 0 0 1 0	B		34	1 0 0 0 1 0	7
3	0 0 0 0 1 1	C		35	1 0 0 0 1 1	8
4	0 0 0 1 0 0	D		36	1 0 0 1 0 0	9
5	0 0 0 1 0 1	E		37	1 0 0 1 0 1	+
6	0 0 0 1 1 0	F		38	1 0 0 1 1 0	−
7	0 0 0 1 1 1	G		39	1 0 0 1 1 1	*
				40	1 0 1 0 0 0	/
	Patterns representing H ⟶ R			41	1 0 1 0 0 1	(
				42	1 0 1 0 1 0	)
				43	1 0 1 0 1 1	£
				44	1 0 1 1 0 0	.
19	0 1 0 0 1 1	S				
20	0 1 0 1 0 0	T				
21	0 1 0 1 0 1	U			Patterns representing additional special characters	
22	0 1 0 1 1 0	V				
23	0 1 0 1 1 1	W				
24	0 1 1 0 0 0	X				
25	0 1 1 0 0 1	Y				
26	0 1 1 0 1 0	Z				
27	0 1 1 0 1 1	0				
28	0 1 1 1 0 0	1				
29	0 1 1 1 0 1	2				
30	0 1 1 1 1 0	3		62	1 1 1 1 1 0	⟶
31	0 1 1 1 1 1	4		63	1 1 1 1 1 1	>

Figure 2.2 Part of an imaginery 64–character set (each character represented by 6 bits). The special characters have particular significance within the use of the various programming languages

character or two decimal digits. In other computers the grouping of bits, bytes or words is flexible in design to meet the differing storage requirements of numbers, alphanumeric characters and instructions.

Information is made up of data and program (instructions). It is stored in the form of alphanumeric data, or as machine instructions. We shall see that in each case the computer word is arranged differently. Let us consider our 36-bit word and see how it relates to the alphanumeric coding. If the alphanumeric data is grouped into 6-bit patterns, one word would contain six characters (figure 2.3).

Numeric data on the other hand uses the entire word since groups of 6-bits would severely restrict the size of numbers. In order to grasp this point fully we must be clear about counting in binary.

Number systems

A number is made up of individual digits (e.g., 803 consists of the digits 8, 0 and 3). The value of each digit in a number is determined by three considerations:

(a) the digit itself;
(b) the position of the digit in the number;
(c) the base of the number system (where base is defined as the number of digits which can occur in any one position).

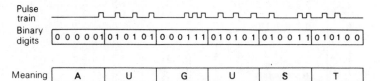

Figure 2.3 Six alphanumeric characters, viz, the bit pattern representation of 'AUGUST' stored in one 36-bit word. The code used is the same one that we built up in figure 2.2. The wavy line above is to indicate the relationship between a 'train' of pulses (how the information is moved about in the machine) and the string of bits it represents. The string is shown with equal spaces between the pulses. The presence of a pulse indicates a 1 bit and the absence of a pulse a 0 bit.

In the decimal system the base is equal to 10 since any position can contain one of ten digits (0 1 2 3 4 5 6 7 8 9). The system therefore has a carrying factor of 10 and each digit indicates a value which depends on the position it occupies:

In 6,421	the digit 6 signifies	6 x 1000
In 4,621	the digit 6 signifies	6 x 100
In 4,261	the digit 6 signifies	6 x 10
In 4,216	the digit 6 signifies	6

Binary number system

In binary, the base is equal to 2 and the two digits are 0 and 1. As we have seen, this system is ideal for coding purposes for the computer because of the two-state nature of the electrical components that are used.

Binary counting

Remember we only have two digits, 0 and 1, and therefore the binary equivalent of the decimal number 2 has to be stated as 10 (a 0 with a 1 carry, read as 'one, zero').

Binary	*Decimal equivalent*
0	0
1	1
10	2
11	3
100	4
101	5
110	6
111	7
1000	8
1001	9
1010	10
1011	11
1100	12
1101	13
1110	14
1111	15

This system has a carrying factor of 2 and each bit has a value which depends on the position it occupies:

In binary:

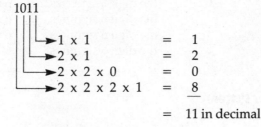

$$
\begin{aligned}
1 \times 1 &= 1 \\
2 \times 1 &= 2 \\
2 \times 2 \times 0 &= 0 \\
2 \times 2 \times 2 \times 1 &= \underline{8} \\
&= 11 \text{ in decimal}
\end{aligned}
$$

In our 36-bit word, numeric data can be represented by up to 35 bits with the 36th bit always reserved to indicate whether the number is positive or negative.

Numbering the bit positions from the right, we can assign each bit a value based on two times the value of the previous bit. The number 1,208,747 is represented in the computer by the unique pattern of 1s and 0s illustrated in figure 2.4. It is the total value of those bits (reading from right to left) marked with a 1 that gives us the number in decimal figures, i.e.:

Bit no.	Value
1	1
2	2
4	8
6	32
8	128
9	256
13	4096
14	8192
15	16384
18	131072
21	1048576
	1208747

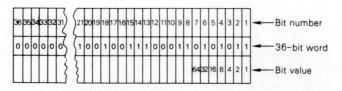

Figure 2.4 A positive number stored in a 36-bit word. A zero sign in bit 36 indicates a positive number, a one sign a negative number

For the purpose of all our computer arithmetic examples we have chosen to work with **integers** (or whole numbers). This is for ease of understanding. In reality, most computer arithmetic is performed on **real numbers,** i.e. numbers expressed with a decimal point (often referred to as **floating point numbers**). The computer word is, of necessity, arranged differently for floating point representation since it needs to accommodate the position of the point as well as the digits. Much larger numbers can be handled when working in floating point form. Floating point arithmetic also provides the accuracy that scientific calculations demand.

THE ARITHMETIC AND LOGIC UNIT (ALU)

This handles both the arithmetic and logical operations on which much of a computer program is based. Before we can think about how circuitry could be designed to handle these functions, we need to have some knowledge of the simplicity of the arithmetic involved.

Computer arithmetic

Addition

We have pointed out how numbers are counted in binary and that numbers are made up of bit patterns only of 1s and 0s. When adding these digits together, the result will also be in 1s and 0s. The following examples indicate all possible combinations of 0 and 1 for addition:

$$
\begin{array}{cccc}
0 & 0 & 1 & 1 \\
+0 & +1 & +0 & +1 \\
\hline
0 & 1 & 1 & 10
\end{array}
$$

Note that the sum of 1 and 1 is written as '10' (a zero sum with a one carry which is the equivalent of the decimal digit '2'.

We can now look at three examples of binary additions which make use of the above combinations:

Example 1

Binary	*Decimal Equivalent*
1 0 1 0	10
+ 1 0 1	+ 5
1 1 1 1	15

Example 2

	Binary		Decimal equivalent
carry	1	carry	1
	1 0 1 0 1 0		42
+	1 0 0 1	+	9
	1 1 0 0 1 1		51

Example 3

	Binary		Decimal equivalent
carry	1 1 1	carry	11
	1 0 1 1 1 0 0 0		184
+	1 1 1 0 1 1	+	59
	1 1 1 1 0 0 1 1		243

In the third example we find a new situation (1 + 1 + 1) brought about by the 1 carry. However, we can still handle this by using the four combinations already mentioned. We add the digits in turn. 1 + 1 = 10 (a 0 sum with a 1 carry). The third 1 is now added to this result to obtain 11 (a 1 sum with a 1 carry).

Our sums have been set down in the traditional manner for human solution. They do not show how the computer adds but they do illustrate the combinations of 1s and 0s that the computer circuitry will have to handle.

The computer performs *all* the other arithmetical operations (x − ÷) by a form of addition. This is easily seen in the case of multiplication, e.g., 5 x 9 may be thought of as essentially being determined by evaluating, with necessary carries, 9 + 9 + 9 + 9 + 9. This idea of repeated addition may seem to be a longer way of doing things, but remember that the computer is designed to perform the operation at great speed. Subtraction and division are handled essentially by addition using the principle of **complementing.**

Complementary subtraction

The computer performs *all* mathematical operations by a form of addition. How can subtraction be achieved using an essentially additive method? The shopkeeper knows how because he does so every time he gives you change. In order to find the right amount of change he merely complements the cost of the purchase up to the sum of money you have offered him. In ordinary (decimal) arithmetic the highest number in any column (units, tens, hundreds, etc.) is 9. The 'nines complement' is that number which, when added to another, makes a total of 9, 99, 999, etc. Hence:

The nines complement of	6	of	10	of	385	
is said to be	3	is	89	is	614	
	9		99		999	

When subtracting by the complementary method three steps are involved:

Step 1 Find the nines complement of the number you are subtracting;

Step 2 Add this to the number from which you are taking away;

Step 3 If there is a carry of 1 add it to obtain the result; if there is no carry add 0, recomplement and attach a negative sign to obtain the result.

Example 1 25 – 10:

Using normal subtraction		*Complementary method*
25		25
−10	Step 1	+89 (nines complement of 10)
15	2	114
	3	►1 (add the carry of 1)
	Result	15

Example 2 14 – 72

Using normal subtraction		*Complementary method*
14		14
−72	Step 1	+27 (nines complement of 72)
−58	2	041
	3	►0 (add 0 as no carry)
		41
	Result	−58 (recomplement and attach a negative sign)

When applied to computer arithmetic, the significance of the complementary method is soon apparent. The binary system only has two digits, therefore subtraction involves 'ones complement'. This is simplicity itself because a reversal of the bits of the binary number provides the ones complement, for example the ones complement of 1001 is 0110.

Let us re-work examples 1 and 2 using binary and the ones complement method.

Example 1   25 – 10:

Binary number		*Complementary method*
11001 (25)		11001
01010 (10)	Step 1	+10101 (ones complement of 01010)
	2	101110
	3	└──▶ 1 (add the carry of 1)
(15)	Result	1111

Example 2   14 – 72:

Binary number		*Complementary method*
0001110 (14)		0001110
1001000 (72)	Step 1	+0110111 (ones complement of 1001000)
	2	01000101
	3	└──▶ 0 (add 0 as no carry)
		1000101
(58)	Result	−0111010 (recomplement and attach a negative sign)

The computer performs the division operation essentially by repeating this complementary subtraction method, e.g. 45 ÷ 9 may be thought of as 45 – 9 = 36 – 9 = 27 – 9 = 18 – 9 = 9 – 9 = 0 (minus 9 *five* times).

We have demonstrated how computer arithmetic is based on addition. Exactly how this simplifies matters can only be understood in the context of binary (not in decimal). The number of individual steps may indeed be increased because all computer arithmetic is reduced to addition, but the computer can carry out binary additions at such great speed that this is not a factor of any significance.

Arithmetic section of the ALU

We have not considered how the computer handles fractions (real numbers) nor have we considered number systems, other than binary, associated with computers, e.g. **octal** (based on eight) and **hexadecimal** (based on sixteen). These two systems are significant because they provide a shorthand notation for expressing binary.

To summarize the basic principles of computer arithmetic it will be seen that:

(a) all forms of arithmetic are handled by a form of addition;
(b) to do this we need to add 1s and 0s to produce other 1s and 0s.

We also need facilities for 'carrying over' and for 'reversing' (to 'complement'). It is not necessary to understand the intricacies of the electronic circuits which are designed to perform these functions, but only that the operations are carried out by means of combinations of signals passing through what are known as 'logic elements' or 'logic gates'.

Logic gates

Circuits are built up using combinations of different types of gates to perform the necessary arithmetic. There are several types of gates, but we shall consider here only three elementary logic gates known as AND, OR and NOT. These are sufficient to introduce the concept of circuit design and to demonstrate the four possible combinations of 1 and 0 in addition.

(a) An AND gate generates an output signal of 1 only if *all* input signals are also 1.

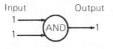
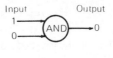
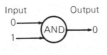
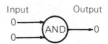

(b) An OR gate generates an output signal of 1 if *any* of the input signals are also 1.

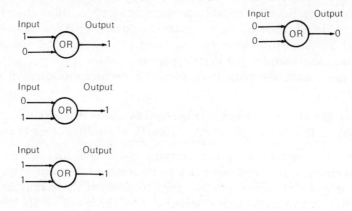

(c) A NOT gate generates an output signal which is the *reverse* of the original signal.

By using the output from one gate as part of the input for another gate, and by using a variety of gates arranged in different sequences, we can build up circuitry to handle arithmetic involving 1s and 0s.

If we reconsider the four possible addition situations we see that the computer must be able to provide for:

$0 + 0$	to produce a	0	sum and a 0 carry
$0 + 1$	to produce a	1	sum and a 0 carry
$1 + 0$	to produce a	1	sum and a 0 carry
$1 + 1$	to produce a	0	sum and a 1 carry

Our need is to produce a series of logic gates which can resolve all four situations correctly, so that whatever the two input signals, the correct sum is always obtained as well as the correct carry (i.e., the *one* circuit works for all). This can be done using two AND gates, one OR and one

NOT, combined in the design illustrated in figure 2.5. Trace any pair of inputs through from A and B and see how the sum and carry are always correct. The first pair (0, 1) has been taken through the total circuit for you and the output signal at each stage indicated.

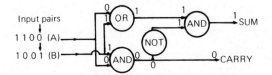

Figure 2.5 Arrangement of gates to add any pair of bits

By linking together designs like this, by using other types of gates that we have not mentioned, and by using gates which can have more than two inputs, we can begin to build up complete circuits which will do all the necessary computer arithmetic operations and be able to work with large strings of bits rather than two at a time.

Logic section of the ALU

The logic gates in the ALU which enable arithmetic to be performed should not be confused with the ability of the computer to handle (test) various conditions occurring during program execution, and to take appropriate action based on the instructions provided by the human programmer. The significance of these logical operations to programming is developed in Chapter Six.

The logical section of the ALU performs all the necessary logical functions, but the details of the circuitry used are beyond the scope of this book.

MEMORY UNIT

The ALU needs data upon which to act and instructions as to how to act. These are obtained from the memory unit which is made up of a number of locations or *cells*. In each of these locations, a word can be stored. A location, therefore, is capable of retaining either an instruction or a piece of data. The number and size of locations in a store (measured in K modules, where K = 1024, remember) varies from machine to machine.

Each is 'numbered' sequentially to provide a unique reference for an item of information held in store. This reference is known as the **location address.**

1025	1030	1035	1040	1045	1050	1055	1060
1026	1031	1036	1041	1046	1051	1056	1061
1027	1032	1037 AUGUST	1042	1047	1052	1057	1062
1028	1033	1038	1043	1048	1053	1058	1063
1029	1034	1039	1044	1049	1054	1059 1,208,747	1064

Figure 2.6 A matrix to represent a small section (locations 1025–1064) of the memory of a hypothetical computer. The number in the top left-hand corner of each cell is the location address (the computer's method of referencing each location). The bit pattern, which according to the context of the program, can be interpreted as 'AUGUST' is stored at location 1037 and the bit pattern representing '1,208,747' is stored at location 1059. Note that the use of a 5 x 8 matrix in this example is not significant – it could just as well have been 40 × 1 or 10 × 4

The purpose of addressing

The concept of addressing is no different from the familiar method of identifying houses in a street. Each house has a number or name, or both, by which it is recognized. It is this unique reference which leads to correspondence (letters, cards, parcels) being delivered to the correct house. The purpose of addressing each location of a computer memory is to identify each cell so that an item of information may be placed in store and thereafter be traced by reference to the location address, which is 'remembered' by the computer. This means the contents of a storage location can be altered and the new information retrieved without the actual contents being known. For example, '19 High Street' is a unique address and Mr Smith may be the present occupant. If Smith leaves and Jones moves in, the postman, like the control unit of the computer, will still continue to deliver correspondence addressed to '19 High Street', irrespective of who the occupant is.

Instructions

In the clerical exercise (earlier in this Chapter) one of the tasks was to make a comparison between a student's mark and the constant pass mark to determine successful and unsuccessful students. This process cannot take place in the memory. It takes place in the arithmetic and logic unit. Before considering this point further it is necessary to examine the basic format of a computer instruction.

An instruction extracted from a word of memory by the control unit normally consists of two parts (see figure 2.7). The operation code is present to signify what has to be done, whilst the address indicates the exact memory location which contains the information to be used when the operation is carried out (executed).

OPERATION (Code)	ADDRESS (Location)

Figure 2.7 Computer instruction

A group of instructions to perform a comparison of a student's mark with the pass mark could be described as follows:

Step 1 Transfer 'pass mark' and 'current student's mark' from store (memory) into the ALU;

Step 2 Compare these two marks;

Step 3a If 'student's mark' is less than 'pass mark' then ignore this mark and move to next 'student's mark';

Step 3b If 'student's mark' is equal to, or greater than, 'pass mark' then add 'student's name and mark' to 'pass list'.

The instructions have been explained in English, of course. In the computer, the instructions have to be defined by **numeric** codes since, as we have seen, all information ends up internally in numeric form. Figure 2.8 illustrates this, but we have used ordinary (decimal) numbers rather than binary for convenience.

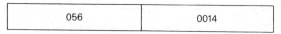

056	0014

Figure 2.8 Computer instruction

If the interpretation of Operation Code 056 is 'add', the example simply states 'add' (to the accumulator; see the section on registers) the contents of the location address '0014' which, remember, is the location of the information, not the information itself.

CONTROL UNIT

It is part of the function of the control unit, once it receives an instruction involving either a calculation or a comparison, to control the movement of data into the ALU and, once the operation has been completed, to move the result to a specified storage location.

If we summarize the computing process we find that the control unit is designed to co-ordinate the representation, storage, and internal movement of instructions and data, as well as the interpretation and subsequent execution of those instructions, and it then has to pass on the results.

Registers

We have noted that there is movement of information within the CPU as each instruction is interpreted and executed. To handle this process satisfactorily it is necessary, at various stages, to retain information on a temporary basis. To do this, the computer uses a number of special memory units called **registers**. They are not considered part of the main memory, and there are several types of register, each designed to perform a specific function. What they have in common is the ability to receive information, to hold it temporarily, and to pass it on as directed by the control unit.

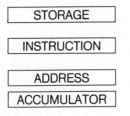

STORAGE	A register that holds information on its way to and from memory.
INSTRUCTION	A register that holds an instruction whilst it is being executed.
ADDRESS	A register that holds a storage location address until it is needed.
ACCUMULATOR	A register that accumulates results.

We hope that, in your brain, your human 'registers' have been at work and that relationships between the ALU, Memory and Control units (the three components of the CPU), are now apparent. We have been concerned with the concepts, the basic principles – the detailed practice of these principles, it will be seen, can soon become very complicated. If these concepts, however, are understood, we can now introduce the idea of a computer installation in which the CPU exists as the centre of all activities.

Your Girlfriend ? —>

A COMPUTER INSTALLATION

We have considered the basic structure of a computer and discovered that it has five functional units. However, in reality it is not as straightforward as this. A computer needs storage space over and above the capacity of its own memory (we recognized this fact in connection with the storage of all the Premium Bond records). The main store of a computer is designed as a working area for a program, i.e., it provides space for the instructions and data (at least for that portion of the data which is currently required), and also space for program manipulation. Information in the memory is retained on a temporary basis only (until the termination of the program). Clearly then, this area of **primary storage** is not the place for information which has to be retained permanently. An area of **secondary storage** is needed for this category of information and this is provided by such auxiliary or 'back-up' storage devices as magnetic disk and magnetic tape.

The input stage of the computing process can be handled by any one of a number of different input devices, e.g., document readers and visual display terminals (keyboard entry). Equally, there are a number of output devices and, of these, the line printer is the one most commonly used. A computer installation may operate using a variety of input/ output devices. These various devices, together with back-up (secondary) storage are discussed in Chapter Four. There may also be a requirement for a communications interface (network processing unit) to provide the physical connection between the central computer and the various terminals remotely situated (not in the computer room) through which people actually communicate with the computer.

Hardware is the jargon term given to the machinery itself and to the various individual pieces of equipment. When the hardware is linked together to form an effective working unit we have a computer

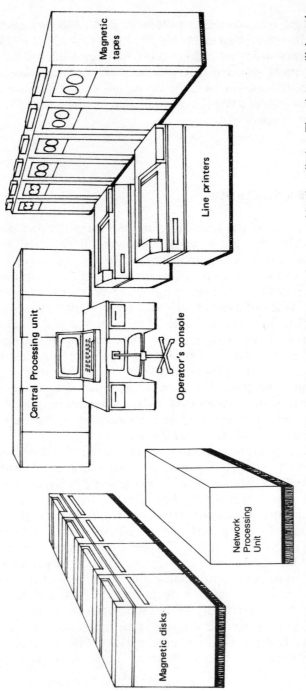

Figure 2.9 A computer installation. The figure shows some of the units which can make up a working installation. The mixture will depend on the work which the installation is intended to support

installation. However, you can do nothing useful with the computer hardware on its own. It has to be driven by certain utility programs, called **software,** which are input and stored permanently in the computer system. The nature and significance of software is developed in Chapter Seven.

3

The Microcomputer

Computers are variously classified as super, mainframe, mini and micro. This classification is based principally on the computer's computing power, i.e., a combination of processing capability and speed, the amount of memory available and, to a lesser degree, the number and types of input/output devices supported. Apart from the difference in physical size, there is a vast difference in the actual cost. Large mainframe systems cost several millions of pounds whereas small micros can be bought for as little as £50.

BASIC STRUCTURE

We are going to look at the microcomputer in some detail because there are some differences in the way in which the various units are organized and assembled compared with traditional computers, as explained in the previous chapter. This is because of the application of microelectronic technology to the design of computers. The structure is a little different but it is important to appreciate that the functions performed are the same. A program which runs or works on a microcomputer could well run on a large mainframe computer without any alteration. The design differences do not therefore affect the computing process.

Microprocessor unit

The advent of the microprocessor followed on from advances in the field of large scale integration (LSI) technology first investigated in the late 1950s. The technology for manufacturing integrated circuits improved over the next twenty years and in 1971 the first microprocessor was produced on a single chip (wafer thin slice) of silicon.[1]

Today, many thousands of components can be built onto a single chip some 5 mm square and no more than 1 mm thick and the density of circuits is increasing all the time. A single chip can contain all the circuitry to perform the combined functions of the control unit and arithmetic/logic unit of the traditionally structured computer (figure 2.1 on page 12). Such a chip is called a **microprocessor unit** (MPU). It is not a complete computer as it lacks memory and input/output capability.

Memory

Memory can be manufactured on a single chip which, like the microprocessor chip, is very small and cheap when produced in large volumes. Individual chips may be mounted on a board to provide some 512K or more memory. Memory may also be assembled on the same chip as the microprocessor and used to control washing machines, cameras, etc. For the purpose of our description the memory is treated as a separate entity. There are four types of memory; each of which is described below.

Random access memory (RAM)

There are various types of memory chips and a single microcomputer might utilize more than one type. The **random access memory** is like the memory of the traditional computer in that information can be read off a RAM chip and written to it. When the computer is switched off, any information stored in RAM is lost. RAM behaves exactly as the central memory described in the previous chapter and would be better called a **read/write memory.**

Read only memory (ROM)

Another type of microcomputer memory is **read only memory**. Information is 'burnt' into the ROM chip at manufacturing time. It cannot be altered and fresh information cannot be 'written' into a ROM. The information can be 'read' and transferred for use elsewhere, for example to a RAM. When the power supply is switched off, the bit patterns in the memory are not lost as they are in the case of the central memory of a computer or a RAM chip.[2] ROMs are used for applications in which it is known that the information never needs to be altered, for example the operating system software (see Chapter Seven) which controls the use of a complete microcomputer system or a monitor program for controlling a washing machine.

Programmable read only memory (PROM)

A variation of the ROM chip is **programmable read only memory.** PROM can be programmed to record information using a facility known as a *prom-programmer*. However, once the chip has been programmed the recorded information cannot be changed, i.e., the PROM becomes a ROM and the stored information can only be 'read'. PROM is also non-volatile storage.

Erasable programmable read only memory (EPROM)

A fourth type of memory is **erasable programmable read only memory.** As the name suggests, information can be erased and the chip programmed anew to record different information using a special prom-programmer facility. Erasure is achieved by exposing the chip to ultraviolet light. When an EPROM is in use in the microcomputer, it behaves like a ROM. In order to erase information and re-program the EPROM, it needs to be taken out of the microcomputer.

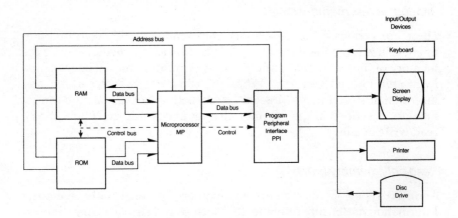

Figure 3.1 A conceptual microcomputer design

TYPES OF MICROCOMPUTER

The single-chip microcomputer

A microcomputer consisting of a microprocessor and some memory can be integrated onto a single chip. This chip is of little use to people who require the services of a centralized computer centre in order to run their payroll, client/job costing, and mailing lists, etc. For such data processing activities, a much more elaborate and, therefore, more expensive microcomputer system is required. On the other hand, the little chip bursting with computer power is ideal for controlling many industrial processes currently performed by electromechanical devices. It is also the basis of pocket calculators.

With a **single-chip microcomputer,** all the functions of the CPU are contained on one small slice of silicon. The microprocessor part provides arithmetic and logic operations and its control unit co-ordinates the activities of a program embedded in a memory chip. This program, designed to perform a specific application, is held in a ROM, PROM or EPROM chip. Via an input device, the ever-changing data for a given application is entered into a RAM. The result from the computer program is handled by an output device. This output device can then, for instance, set the spin program for a washing machine or set an alarm going or control the fuel injection in a vehicle. Already, some 20,000 potential industrial and process control applications have been identified.

The advantages of microchip computers are a reduction in cost and size of components, increase in performance and reliability and scope for innovation. Most industrial and process firms can now afford to purchase computing power. Even though it may be possible, economically, to improve existing methods without computers, the point has been reached where firms failing to employ computer power could easily lose out to competitors.

A microcomputer on a chip can cost between £5 and £50. To keep to this low cost per unit, however, they must be produced in large numbers. Software skills are required to produce the program which will make the chip function in the correct way; engineering skills are also needed to interface the basic chip to input and output devices.

By placing a new program in the EPROM chip, or by exchanging the ROM or PROM chip with another one with a different program, the microchip computer is happy to perform a different task.

The multi-board microcomputer system

The single-chip computer, depending on its complexity and degree of speciality, is suited to applications such as process control, instrumentation and communications. Many other applications require far greater computer facilities than those offered by the single-chip; data-processing and commercial applications are such areas. In these cases, there is a need for much more sophisticated input/output devices than the limited entry buttons and display panel of the pocket calculator type.

All these **peripheral devices** need to be connected to the microcomputer in order to form a computer hardware system. Such a system will need system software to drive the hardware units, as well as application programs to perform specific data processing tasks.

Usually, the input/output device is a VDU (visual display unit) where the keyboard acts as the input device and the cathode ray tube screen acts as the output display device. A printer will also be required for permanent copies if required. Storage for data, application programs, and for certain operating system software which cannot be held in ROM, is provided by some form of mass storage device, such as a floppy disk and hard disk system.

Another important aspect of microcomputer systems is the **operating system.** Currently, many different hardware systems exist. With the increase in the development of packages for use on microcomputers involving a relatively high capital investment, attempts to standardize operating systems make sense. A package designed for use on a given operating system rather than on a given hardware system will be cheaper since the market will be larger. CP/M (Control Program for Microcomputers) became the standard for the 8-bit micro; MS-DOS, PC-DOS are common systems for 16-bit microprocessors.

The first generation of commercially available micros was based on the use of 8-bit microprocessors (e.g. Zilog's Z-80), i.e., the MPU was limited to 8-bit registers such as the accumulator. The memory chips were also 8-bit devices. Current systems employ 16-bit (e.g. Intel's 80286) and 32-bit (e.g. Motorola's MC68020) microprocessors and it is these more powerful micros which provide minicomputer capability at microcomputer prices.

A microcomputer is often designed so that it can be **configured** with different sizes of RAM, typically, in the range 64K – 512K RAM. A 64K RAM can be expanded to a 512K RAM by adding on additional 64K RAM chips or by exchanging a memory board for one with a higher capacity. This concept of add on and replacement boards is fundamental to the design of many microcomputers. It enables one version, probably at the cheap end of the market, to be enhanced (made more powerful) by adding on extra memory, etc, yet allowing the user to continue to use programs and data in the same manner as before. Likewise, faults can be remedied quickly by replacing a complete unit with another. Maintenance by replacement is feasible because of the comparatively low cost involved.

A microcomputer is usually equipped with a typewriter keyboard for input and can normally be linked to a CRT (cathode ray tube) monitor for display of input and output. A terminal printer may also be connected to provide printed copy of output on paper. Fully configured systems (figure 3.2) include floppy disk drives and possibly hard disks which collectively provide extra and permanent storage. These various forms of storage are described together with input/output devices in the next chapter. Further discussion about microcomputer technology can be found in Appendix One.

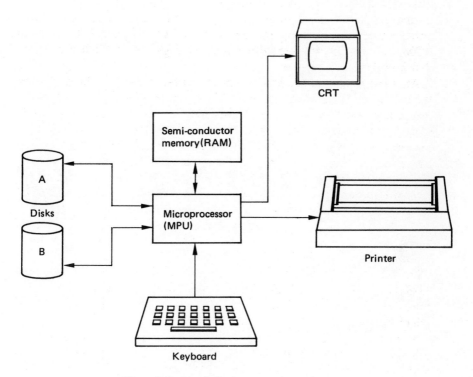

Figure 3.2 A typical microcomputer system

NOTES

1 Silicon is an element of sand and a naturally poor conductor of electricity. By chemical process the surface and interior of the chip is given electronic qualities and the required pattern of circuits is established by a photoetching process.

2 Memories which retain information after the power has been switched off so that it is still present when the power is switched on again are termed *non-volatile* memories. Those which lose information when the power is switched off are called *volatile*.

4

The Human–Computer Interface

The first electronic computer was completed in 1946, but it was not until the mid-fifties that there was a computer industry as such. Since that time, aided by new technology, the industry has made phenomenal progress. For example, notable advances have occurred in processor speeds and the provision of storage. These in turn have facilitated the development of sophisticated computer systems and complex software. Operating systems are discussed in detail in Chapter Seven and applications packages in Chapter Nine. Future developments read like a science-fiction story with powerful computers shrunk to the size of a match-box. However, there is one area which, comparatively speaking, has not developed to the same extent. This is the realm of 'man to machine' and 'machine to man' communication, in other words, the input/output devices. The principal reason for this is that, here, speed of communication depends in many cases on mechanical movement and the potential for improvement of such devices is limited.

Input/output units surround the central processor, hence the term *peripheral devices*. Their purpose is to provide an information link between the outside world and the CPU. In computing parlance, they act as an *interface*, translating the familiar symbols which we can read into the binary patterns that can be handled electronically within the CPU: they then translate the patterns back again for easily readable or pictorial output.

INPUT

Communicating with computers has always been a problem. In the early days, programmers had to communicate directly with the computer in its own language. People, rather than the machine, had to do the translating. The difficulties of having to think in binary led to the development of easier methods of communication. In some cases the operator was able to do this by making use of existing technology from other fields. For example, the use of punched cards and perforated tape by people unfamiliar with binary permitted the encoding of our familiar symbols into an intermediate stage. This intermediate stage was then translated, by the machine, into binary.

During the first twenty years of the commercial use of computers, communication was based principally on the employment of punched cards and, to a lesser extent, paper tape. Information, depicted by holes punched on the media, was passed to the computer via a special reading device, with each character represented by a unique pattern of holes. More direct and convenient methods of communication have since evolved and today the punched card is essentially a feature of the past, although its influence on computing lingers on in a variety of ways.[1]

Keyboard entry of data is now the main method of input. There are two principal categories of keyboard device: the teletypewriter terminal (like a typewriter) and the visual (TV-type) display device equipped with a keyboard for input, known as a VDU.[2] More recent developments are hand-held terminal entry systems and hand-print pads. Developments have also taken place which permit the computer to 'read' typed (and even written) symbols directly, via **optical mark reading** (OMR), **magnetic ink character recognition** (MICR) and **optical character recognition** (OCR) (see pages 43–7). In addition, research into voice input has been successful enough for some commercial companies to use this method of communication in a limited way.

Terminals

Teletypewriter terminal A teletypewriter terminal, sometimes called a teleprinter terminal or a keyboard/printer terminal, usually combines a keyboard for manual input of information with a printer for outputting a 'hard copy' (printed record) of the input, system information and program results. The printing device outputs one character at a time at rates of 20 to 80 characters per second on continuous rolls of paper (typically 8 to 20 in wide) or on fanfold paper, according to the application. VDUs are the most common form of terminal – the information is displayed on the screen as it is typed.

One of the features of a terminal is that it can be situated some distance from the computer. It must, therefore, include some means of transmitting information. Some terminals are designed only to send information and some only to receive, but usually both functions are carried out.

Terminals may be connected to a computer in one of two ways. Some are connected *locally*, by direct cable lines. This is known as 'hard-wiring' and does not usually extend more than several hundred feet from the computer itself. The second method is via a *remote* link, either by telegraph, telephone line,[3] network[4] or by microwaves. Whilst it is probable that the remote terminal would be some distance from the computer, it is possible that it may be on the same site as the computer, even in the same room. The terms *local* and *remote* refer to the *way* in which a terminal is linked to the computer rather than to *distance*, i.e. it is *directly* connected (hard-wired), or *indirectly* connected through other means. Both methods permit the simultaneous linking of several terminals in several locations to the one computer, with each terminal making use of the computer in turn. This is known as **time sharing,** a concept which is developed in some detail in Chapter Seven.

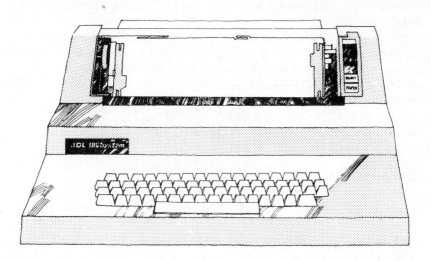

Figure 4.1

Terminals extend the use of the computer to various places of work. They are widely used for such tasks as stock control, entering orders, updating accounts and seat reservations. The terminals found in shops and stores (point-of-sale terminals) might combine several of these tasks whilst also acting as cash registers. They can be sited at various points on a factory floor to record and receive information on different stages of an industrial process. The development of compact portable terminals has extended their usefulness still further.

Terminals provide an extremely important and effective communication link with the computer. Their versatility, combined with the fact that they can be situated away from the computer, has led to a rapid growth in their use, and they are now the standard input device in most applications.

Most modern terminals contain circuitry and software that allows some computing tasks to be performed without contact with a central computer, e.g., editing data and text. Terminals which can carry out such assignments are often referred to as **intelligent terminals**. The degree of local intelligence given to terminals is expanding.

Bar-code recognition   Lines or bars can be arranged in a code as illustrated in figure 4.2. Bar-codes are used particularly by the retail trade for labelling goods, and by supermarkets for labelling shelves and in stock control. They are also used for numbering books in public libraries, so that when a book is borrowed or returned it can be recorded using a computer.

Bar-code reading is performed by a scanner or light pen which is generally linked to a computer via a terminal device. The scanner or light pen is stroked across the pattern of bars, a sequence of bits is generated and the information recorded.

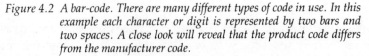

Figure 4.2   A bar-code. There are many different types of code in use. In this example each character or digit is represented by two bars and two spaces. A close look will reveal that the product code differs from the manufacturer code.

Hand-held terminal   Another innovation is the development of the **hand-held data entry terminal**. A typical hand-held device looks similar to a calculator and is normally battery powered for use in the field. Information is usually entered via keys and the device may incorporate a display panel that enables a line of data to be viewed as it is entered. In addition, a scanner or light pen may be attached to enable capture of bar-coded data. A certain amount of memory (up to about 64K) is normally provided for temporary storage of data before transmission to a computer. Typically, the transmission is through ordinary telephones, in which case an acoustic coupler is required to connect the terminal to the telephone. Some hand-held terminals can be connected to cassette tape recorders for the purpose of storing data.

The hand-held device enables the collection of data at the place where it is generated and avoids the delay and cost of data preparation at the computer site. The hand-held terminal could be useful to a salesman in the field for direct ordering, or for such applications as meter reading, road traffic surveys, control of medical supplies in hospitals and production line monitoring.

Even the hand-held terminal can be endowed with some intelligence, enabling a device to be set up for a particular application, so that, for example, it prompts the operator for the next input and perhaps runs an initial check on the validity of data as it is input. For applications in the field where immediate computed results are required as well as the capture of data, completely self-contained hand-held portable micro-computers[5] can be used.

Hand-print terminal   A recent development is the introduction of **hand-print** terminals, variously called *data tablets* or *pads*. The device generates a representation of a character direct to the computer as the character is hand-printed on paper lying on top of the pad. Different types of pad employ different sensing techniques and a special pen is sometimes required. One method is based on the generation of pulses when two electrically resistive layers beneath the surface of the pad are brought together by the pressure of the pen as the characters are printed. A typical data pad incorporates a touch sensitive keyboard for entering non-written characters. It may also be able to digitize, and hence input, drawings as well as characters.

Mark and character recognition

The method involves the recognition of marks or characters, e.g. from work dockets, cheques, sales order entry forms and even printed text. There are three types of recognition:

- **optical mark reading** (OMR)
- **magnetic ink character recognition** (MICR)
- **optical character recognition** (OCR)

The general point to note is that these forms of recognition facilitate the direct transfer of data from source document to the electronic form in which information is held in the computer. Where they are used they eliminate the need for the laborious key-entry of data that is associated with terminal and key-to-disk and key-to-tape systems.[6]

Optical mark reading   Forms and cards are pre-printed for special purposes so that a mark can be made in a specified position, for example to represent a yes or no answer in a market survey, or in a combination of positions to indicate different characters or the different digits of a number in connection for example, with gas and electricity meter readings.

Optical mark readers are now able to scan forms completed in pen or biro, as well as in pencil. The forms or cards are passed under a light source and the presence of a mark is detected by measuring very accurately the infra-red light levels. A mark reader may be able to detect coloured marks. It may also be designed to be insensitive to certain colours so that these particular colours can be used safely in the pre-printing of the documents or cards without risk of their being read as marks intended for recognition. A well-designed form provides a versatile and efficient means of collecting data and the great advantage of OMR is that no specialist skills are required to collect and input data. Data collection can be practised at the point at which the information first becomes available, e.g., on the factory floor, in the warehouse and on the building site.

Another form of mark reading relies on the conductivity of graphite marks. The method necessitates the use of a soft pencil, and non-graphite pen or printed marks are not acceptable. It is known as **mark sense reading** (as opposed to OMR). The early developments in mark reading were of this type. Today mark sensing has been largely superseded by OMR.

Magnetic ink character recognition   Due to the success of mark recognition, investigation turned to the possibility of *reading* characters. The first successful form of character recognition was in the area of MICR. This system uses highly stylized character shapes printed in an ink containing magnetizable particles. Early in 1966, two standard MICR fonts (typographical styles) were accepted by the International Standards Organization. One, known as E13B, consists of the numerals 0–9 and four special characters. This is used principally for bank cheques.

The code number of the bank, the customer's account number, and the cheque sequence number are all pre-printed in magnetic ink. When a cheque is submitted to a bank, the amount of the transaction is enscribed on it before the cheque is presented for computer processing.

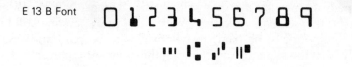

Fig. 4.3 Magnetic ink character recognition fonts

The magnetized ink induces a current in a reading circuit. The current induced will be proportional to the area of ink being scanned. The patterns of the varying currents can then be compared with, and identified as, bit patterns of the selected character. E13B is used in the USA, where it originated, and in the UK. Another MICR font, which originated in France and is used in Europe, is CMC7. This includes the digits 0–9, the letters of the alphabet, and five special characters. The symbols are made up of seven magnetizable lines with six spaces of varying width between them. A wide space generates a binary 1, a narrow space a 0. We saw in Chapter Two the variations that are possible with 6-bit patterns (see figure 2.2). The speed of reading MICR is around 1200 documents a minute.

MICR systems employ character styles designed expressly for machine recognition and, therefore, the characters have to be accurately formed. They also require magnetic ink. These factors make for expensive printing, but one useful advantage is that characters printed with ink containing magnetizable particles can still be read even when over-stamped, as may be the case with bank cheques. MICR readers cannot verify, they can only identify. With a cheque, someone still has to verify the amount to be paid, to whom it is to be paid and, most importantly, that the signature authorizing the payment is correct.

Optical character recognition   It is not only hand-writing which varies. Different typewriters and different typesetters produce the letters of the alphabet in a variety of forms, shapes and sizes. Nevertheless, there are certain characteristics which are peculiar to, and common to, each letter, however it is produced.

OCR readers, or **scanners** as they are sometimes called, typically examine each character as if it were made up of a collection of minute spots (figure 4.4). Once the whole character has been scanned, the pattern detected is matched against a set of patterns stored in the computer. Whichever pattern it matches, or nearly matches, is considered to be the character read. Patterns which cannot be identified are rejected.

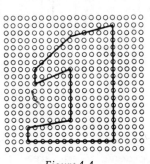

Figure 4.4

There is now an extensive range of OCR equipment on the market from scanners that plug into humble personal computers to sophisticated data entry machines that ultilize quite powerful minicomputer systems. The more powerful devices can handle many different character fonts in various point (character) sizes, and they can also generally operate in a 'teach mode' which enables them to learn any specific font that is required.

A typical small scanner looks like a miniature drawing board with a rule that slides up and down a rail on the left hand side of the device. Read heads are positioned in a small box which slides, under manual guidance, from left to right over the line of text immediately above the rule. Such a scanner may be equipped to identify as many as four different (but commonly used) type faces (fonts) with the capability to learn an additional font of the user's choice. A typical line scan takes between one and three seconds to complete.

A powerful data entry system is capable of reading multifont text (printed books and typewritten manuscripts). Rather than retaining all the different type faces that may be needed at one time or another, these systems are designed to learn (using teach or training mode) all about the shapes of the characters of the various fonts specific to the document that needs to be read. Data entry, the actual reading or scanning process, only commences when training is complete. The training process is carried out under manual supervision and involves the operator answering a menu of questions about the typeface in question. Such OCR devices may be able to convert texts in both Roman and non-Roman alphabets into machine-readable form (typically output to magnetic tape for subsequent use) and can operate in data entry mode at 300 or more words per minute. Speed of reading is relatively low because of the need for accuracy, but it is considerably faster than keyboard entry which OCR readers are designed to replace. However, whatever the level of sophistication of the device, the quality of reading depends directly on the quality of the text which is being scanned.

It is possible that a computer could be programmed to accept *some* signatures, but it is unlikely that it could ever be programmed to accept every type of signature. Even so, devices have been developed which can read *neat* hand printing (capital letters rather than lower case) in black ink, and with sufficient accuracy for this to become a viable form of input.

Voice-Input

A voice-input system accepts spoken input. The waveform created by the spoken input is analysed, patterns are extracted and matched against prestored patterns to identify the input. Once identified, the appropriate coding is generated for handling within the computer. Before a voice-input system can be used it must first be provided with a vocabulary. The words and phrases the system is to recognize are spoken with the system operating in a so-called 'training mode'. In this mode, the patterns are created and stored for future matching. A system may be trained to recognize both the voice of one or more operators and a given vocabulary for each operator, in which case unwanted inputs or unauthorized speakers are rejected.

The voice link to a system may be by microphone, telephone or radio communication. Voice-input systems are not yet widely used but they are a reality. Vocabularies are comparatively small, typically 100 to 300 words. In general, as the size of a vocabulary increases, recognition reliability decreases. Possible applications are situations in which an operator needs to be free to move about a work area or to have his hands free, or where an operator travels and relies on telephone contact with his work base.

OUTPUT

We have seen that there are several paths by which humans can communicate with computers. There are also several ways in which the machine can communicate with man.

At one time all that appeared to matter was obtaining results from the computing process and no one bothered very much about presentation of the material. However, it is now becoming increasingly important to present information in the best possible fashion and the industry is responding by placing greater emphasis on improving peripheral type devices (display terminals as well as those providing hard copy output). The provision of quality output is an area of research and development and recently great improvements have been made.

Printed output

Printing techniques can be divided into two major categories: devices that strike a ribbon to deposit ink or carbon onto paper (**impact printers**) and those which do not (**non-impact printers**). Printers can also be categorized in another way: those which output one character at a time (**serial printers**) and those which output a complete line at a time (**line and page printers**).

Serial printers These printers output one character at a time as opposed to one line at a time, e.g. a teletypewriter terminal printer. Some devices are print-only machines with no keyboard for input purposes. A serial printing device can normally be operated using continuous stationery or separate sheets, typically A4 size. A serial or character printer is much slower than a line printer. It is also much cheaper.

A special type is the *daisywheel printer*, so called because it uses a daisy-shaped disk made of metal or plastic which holds some 96 characters on its 'petals'. Print heads are physically interchangeable, enabling the use of different character fonts. There are normally 132 or 136 print positions per line and typical printing speeds are 25 to 60 characters per second (cps). Daisywheel printers are noted for their high print quality and are often used with word processing systems (see page 112) and other applications where letter quality printing is desired.

The *dot matrix printer* is the most common type of serial printer in use. This is because of its speed, versatility, and ruggedness. These qualities, combined with low cost, make the matrix printer particularly attractive to the personal computer market. The print head comprises a matrix of tiny needles which hammers out characters in the form of patterns of tiny dots. The shape of each character, i.e., the dot pattern, is obtained from information held electronically.

Matrix printers are faster than daisywheel printers in the range 50 to 480 cps but in general the quality of print is inferior. There are, however, some devices at the top end of the range with higher-density printheads (18 and 24-pin) which can provide print quality roughly equal to that of a daisywheel printer though this is achieved at the expense of speed. The versatility of some matrix devices is such that they can operate in different print modes: draft mode (high speed, i.e. 200–480 cps); near-letter quality mode (up to 180 cps); or letter quality mode (50–75 cps). Some of the latest dot matrix printers can also output in colour (graphics and alphanumeric characters).

In addition, there are devices which employ non-impact techniques. *Thermal matrix printers* use heated print elements to create characters in dot matrix form on special sensitized paper or on special ribbon from which the required character images are transferred to plain paper. The technology permits a smaller dot size than is attainable with impact dot matrix devices and hence offers higher print resolution, typically 200 dpi. Thermal matrix printers are very quiet in operation but are relatively slow. The method of printing means that the creation of multiple copies is not possible. It also requires special paper, or ribbon which increases printing costs.

Serial printers are suitable for applications producing low volume output and are frequently used as output devices for small, special-purpose computer systems and microcomputers.

Line printer A common method of obtaining bulk output is via a device known as a line printer. Rows of character sets (fonts) are either wrapped around a drum or affixed to a chain. The drum or chain revolves across the path of a series of hammers, each of which corresponds to a print position. As the character to be printed is selected, a magnetically controlled hammer presses it onto an ink ribbon and thence onto paper, rather like a typewriter. A complete line is printed in one 'print cycle'.

A variety of stationery is used, with special designs to suit particular applications, such as pre-printed electricity bills and rate demands. Forms can also be multi-part (where copies are required for different departments), with several sheets impregnated with carbon or separated by interleaved carbon paper. In general, though, the paper used on drum and chain line printers is known as 'continuous stationery'. The paper can be plain or lined, is usually fan-folded and perforated for separation into convenient lengths (11 in typically and about 15 in wide) and comes folded in boxes, usually in ream (500) multiples.

There are normally 132 or 136 print positions per line though some devices are able to print more. Character sets vary in content and size. The 64-set has more special characters than the 48-set and the 96-set prints in lower-case letters as well as in upper-case (capitals). It is even possible to print in Hebrew and in Japanese. The impact (letterpress) method of printing employed by line printers has limitations with respect to quality but it allows for very high speeds, ranging from 300 to 2500 lines per minute (lpm) and is associated particularly with large computer output requirements.

Chain and drum devices for long dominated the line printer market but dot matrix, thermal transfer and ink jet technologies (see below) are now competing strongly. In particular the dot matrix line printer is growing in importance. The technology offers greater flexibility (graphics and multifont capability) and at a lower cost it is particularly attractive for applications where speeds of 600 lpm and below are adequate.

Laser printers   The most important and exciting recent development is the **laser printer** (sometimes referred to as a page or document printer). Using a combination of laser and photocopier technology, these printers are capable of converting computer output into print, page by page. Laser printers produce very high quality images (graphics and text), generally offer a wide selection of character fonts (typically ten or more), are very quiet and operate very quickly. They are more expensive than most other types but there are devices at the bottom end of the market cheap enough to be aimed specifically at personal computer users. These so-called desk or table top laser printers are typically capable of producing 8 *pages* per minute (ppm).

Laser printers are sometimes classified in terms of their speed and cost. Those in the upper bracket provide copy at the rate of 120 to 300 ppm, may have 80 or more selectable fonts and produce near typeset quality. Such top-of-the-range devices may be justifiable for very high volume and specialized applications. Those in the middle range operate at speeds of 40 to 110 ppm, and those in the bottom group at 8 to 36 ppm. A print resolution of 300 dpi is standard but some devices offer even higher resolution and can create colour images.

At the heart of a laser printer there is, in essence, a computer to orchestrate the display of information (complex graphics images as well as text) in the variety of forms possible. In particular, storage space is required to house the volume of output transferred to the device for printing a page at a time, and also for retaining patterns of the extensive range of characters and different fonts. Even a desk-top device in the bottom bracket may be equipped with as much as 1.5 Mb of RAM and yet still have a requirement for plug-in font cartridges.

Ink jet printer   The **ink jet printer** is another non-impact type. Ink droplets are squirted onto paper from nozzles to form characters using the dot matrix principle. Plain paper can be used and the print operation is very quiet. The range of devices is wide and the technology continues to improve. At the top end of the range there are machines capable of generating colour images of near photographic quality with resolution approaching 300 dpi, operable in letter quality or draft mode.

New developments in page printing involve the making of images with magnets, termed **magnetographic printing**, and the use of **LCS** (liquid crystal shutter) technology. Magnetographic printing offers the potential of quality page printing at reasonable cost.

Visual display units (VDU)

A visual display device uses a cathode ray tube (CRT) to display information. It looks like a television screen and is similar in other respects (see figure 4.5). VDUs are particularly useful in situations where information is required quickly and where perhaps there is little advantage in having a permanent record of the information.

The VDU is a type of terminal, with a keyboard for manual input of characters to the computer and a screen for character display of the input or output. It is now the most widely used type of terminal. The screen displays information as it is keyed in enabling a visual check before the input is transferred to the computer.[7] The VDU is extensively used for keyboard entry of data. Information is displayed very much more quickly than by the conventional keyboard/printer terminal

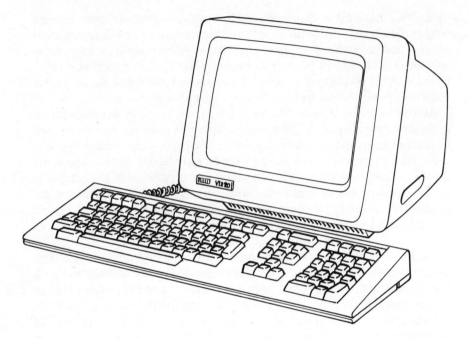

Figure 4.5 A typical visual display unit

(teletypewriter) and it is almost silent in operation. One disadvantage is that the device provides no 'hard' copy of the output, but it is normally possible to add a printing device which can be brought into operation to provide a 'hard' copy of the display when it is needed. However, in the type of applications for which VDUs are particularly suited, where the display provides information on which action is taken immediately, there is often no requirement for printed output.

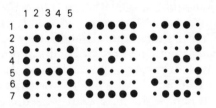

Figure 4.6 A matrix five dots wide by seven dots high (5 × 7), is illustrated in this example. VDUs using a 7 × 9 dot matrix are also common

The most common display method is to generate characters from a 'dot matrix'. A selected pattern of dots is illuminated to form a character (figure 4.6). Screens vary in size (12 in and 14 in are common) and in the number of characters which they can display. A maximum display is typically 24 lines of 80 characters, with sometimes an optional display of 132 characters per line.

Initially used in situations where information is required quickly, for example in airline seat reservations where speed is the essence in handling customer enquiries, VDUs are now widely used for general data entry and retrieval of stored information. The VDU is fast becoming as common a piece of office equipment as the typewriter. Many of today's models are intelligent terminals, incorporating microprocessors, and able to carry out some computing functions. Typically, there are a set of keys on the keyboard, in addition to the 'qwerty' set and other special characters associated with computer keyboards, that can be programmed (set up) to perform tasks at a single keystroke. These so-called **programmable function keys** can make the terminal easier to use by reducing the number of keystrokes for common tasks or they can assist more directly in the user's particular application.

Video screens display white characters on a black background but amber or green displays (rather than white) are also common. VDUs can also operate with colour monitors, and, as the technology improves and costs fall, so use of colour is becoming more common. Most modern VDUs are endowed with a limited graphics capability as well, or this is a feature that can be added by the addition of a **graphics board**.

Some VDUs are equipped with **touch sensitive screens** which allow data to be input by touching the screen with the fingertip. The screen surface consists of a number of 'touch points' as defined by the program in use. When touched, the terminal sends the co-ordinates of the point to the computer. The **mouse** provides another alternative to keyboard entry. It is a hand-held 'pointing' device that is moved around in any direction on a flat surface (i.e., your desk) and in so doing produces a corresponding movement of an electronic pointer or **cursor** on the screen of the VDU. When the cursor is where it is wanted (pointing at the spot you wish to control in some way) the required action is instigated by pressing a button on the back of the mouse. The movement and actions triggered by the mouse are directly related to the software in use.[8]

Graphics

Information can be output in graphical form using graph plotters. These are slow compared with other forms of output but the compensation is a very high degree of accuracy (up to within one thousandth of an inch). In plotting, accuracy is more important than speed. Since there is a considerable mismatch between the speed at which the CPU operates and the speed of the plotting device, output is often transferred to magnetic tape first, and then plotted from the information on the tape. Computer systems dedicated to supporting applications where graphical output is of the utmost significance, e.g., in design, may send output direct to a plotter.

The most common type of plotter is the **flat bed** device. As the name suggests, it plots on paper (or some other material) which rests on a flat bed. The pen moves in perpendicular directions across the bed. One directional movement is supplied by a gantry which straddles the bed and runs on rails at either side. The rails allow movement up and down the length of the bed. The other direction is supplied by a pen turret running to and fro across the gantry itself. The turret may contain different coloured pens (felt tip, ball-point or ink) for multi-coloured plotting. The plot size is restricted by the area of the bed. Some may be small, desk-top devices plotting A2 size whilst very large beds used in aircraft design, for such things as wing profiles, can be up to 20ft by 50ft. Plotters are used to trace out conventional graphs and to assist with design, e.g., in textiles. Some plotters can etch plastic or metal plates.

Another type of plotter is the **drum plotter**. The plotting paper is fed round a drum which revolves in both directions (back and forth). The pen turret is suspended from a bar above the drum and moves from side to side, plotting or moving to a new position, as the drum revolves at right angles to the bar.

Ink jet technology is now beginning to compete with the traditional form of graph plotting described above for some applications. Ink jet colour copiers are ideal for providing hard copy from the brilliantly colourful and intricately detailed displays that can be obtained on state-of-the-art graphical display devices. They are particularly suited to the production of business graphs, statistical plots and technical drawings which do not depend on quite the same degree of accuracy that a flat bed plotter can provide.

Graphics VDU   This type of VDU is specifically designed to display graphics and diagrams as well as alphanumeric characters. The graphics VDU is a specialized piece of equipment, normally very much more expensive than the conventional VDU, and it is used, for example, to support CAD (computer-aided design) applications such as electronics engineering, mechanical drafting and structural analysis. Given the appropriate software, designs can be viewed from different angles and any specific detail highlighted and displayed at varying levels of magnification. The design can then be modified as necessary. Designs may be enhanced by different shades of grey but the emphasis today is on colour monitors and colour graphics.

Graphics can make considerable programming demands on a system and the sophisticated types of display are often linked to large, powerful computer systems, or to smaller machines which are used solely for this one purpose.[9] In addition, most graphics terminals feature resident intelligent graphics routines which enable some of the tasks to be performed locally, sharing the overall computational process associated with computer graphics with the computer. Such intelligent terminals are referred to as work stations.

Screen sizes vary, but 14 in and 19 in are common. Screen resolution which directly controls the level and accuracy of detail of the display also varies, ranging from 640 x 480 **pixels**[10] at the lower end of the market to 1280 x 1024 at the upper end. A colour device can typically display in 16 different colours whilst some of the up-market devices offer 256 different colours (or shades of colours).[11]

A copying device can be used in conjunction with a graphics VDU to provide hard copy of any display. A link up with a **computer output microfilm** (COM) device (see below) can be particularly appropriate. It enables the recording of a whole series of graphs or designs which can then be viewed at leisure to assist, for example, in the selection of an optimum design.

Computer output microfilm (COM)

A computer output microfilm device translates information normally held on magnetic tape into miniature images on microfilm. The device displays the information as characters on a CRT screen and then using photographic methods records the display onto film, usually 16 or 35 mm.[12] Drawings or pictures can usually be displayed as well as narrative text. A full display (perhaps equivalent to a page of line printer output) is recorded as a single frame.

A special reader or reader/printer can be used subsequently to view the processed film. The reader operates on a 'back projection' principle displaying a frame at a time on a translucent screen, typically about A4 size. The printer can then if required, produce a hard copy of what is presented on the screen probably using an electrostatic method.

Microfilm, in roll form or **microfiche,** is small and easily stored and the speed of recording is some 25–50 times faster than the average line printer. The equivalent of thousands of pages of computer output can be stored in a small drawer and the cost of the microfilm for a page of output is less than a sheet of line printer paper. Once the film has been processed it can easily be duplicated and full-size hard copy prints can be made quickly and inexpensively.

A COM system is ideal for use in applications where there is a large amount of information to be retained which is required only for reference purposes such as technical manuals, industrial catalogues and archives. Companies may need to retain records of such things as bills and invoices for a number of years before destroying them. COM provides an easy way of retaining information, of retrieving it in a matter of seconds using a compact desk-top viewer and is ideal when multiple copies of reports or information are required. The information may be distributed in microfiche form.

Complete COM systems are relatively expensive to install and are associated more with big computer users. Small and medium-sized computer users who need microfilm are more likely to take their files for conversion into microfilm to a bureau offering a COM processing service. Desk-top microfiche readers, ideal for use on workshop benches as well as in offices, are comparatively inexpensive. There are also portable readers small enough to fit into briefcases which run off mains or batteries.

Information on microfilm can also be input directly to a computer using CIM (**computer input microfilm**) equipment. This is a relatively new area of development which is receiving increasing attention. At concept level, a CIM system retrieves the relevant roll of film from its 'film library', selects the correct frame, digitizes the document stored on the frame and displays the image on a screen. The digitized document can then be transferred to disk storage for subsequent processing or straight to memory for immediate attention. CIM developments typically make use of the new optical-disk technology (see page 64) benefiting from the enormous capacity that these devices offer. CIM is potentially useful in applications that need to archive large volumes of data for possible or occasional reference some time in the future (e.g. paid accounts and insurance documents).

Audio response units

The computer can be used to trigger verbal communication via an audio response unit and this could be an appropriate method to use if standard replies to requests for information are all that are required.

Messages are composed and transmitted in coded form, maybe over telephone lines, perhaps using a keyboard for input or even a voice-input system. The unit analyses the input, assembles the response from pre-recorded words and phrases, and delivers the verbal reply. For the sake of clarity, the response is delivered more slowly than words are normally spoken. The digitized format in which the spoken word is retained by the system makes heavy demands on storage and typical systems can only store around 400 spoken words or phrases. However, within the context of a single application, the limitation of a small vocabulary may not be unduly restrictive.

Speech synthesis is getting cheaper and voice output is starting to make sense in a variety of applications. Transient information, that is information which only needs to be conveyed once, may be a good candidate for voice output. A good test of whether information is transient is whether it can usefully be conveyed over the telephone. Potential application areas include remote enquiry of product availability, and instructional sequences for various procedures. An audio response unit, sometimes called a voice output terminal may be attached to a large computer system or be supported by a minicomputer perhaps dedicated to the one purpose. Very small devices in the form of micro-chips or boards can be added to some microsystems to provide limited voice output, for example, with spelling instruction and learning games.

BACKING STORES

We indicated earlier that a computer's memory is limited in size, is needed as a working space for the current program, and only retains information on a temporary basis (Chapter Two, page 29). However, computers may often work on vast amounts of data and backing stores are used to retain the data on a permanent basis. Information stored on these devices can be retrieved and transferred speedily to the CPU when it is required.

Several different devices can provide this additional storage space, but the one selected will depend mainly on how the information needs to be accessed. There are two methods of access: *serial* and *direct*. Information on a serial device can only be considered in the same sequence in which it is stored. This would be suitable, for example, for dealing with a mailing list where each address needs to be accessed in turn. However, should an address be required out of order, it can only be retrieved by searching through all those addresses which are stored before it. More often, we need to access information in a more direct manner than serial devices allow. For example, at any given moment in a bank, some customer will be requesting details about his or her account. Backing storage devices exist which permit access to individual information in this more direct or immediate manner. Each item of information held on this type of store is associated with a location address, in much the same way that information is held in the main memory. These direct devices are also called random access devices because the information is literally available at random, i.e., it is available in any order.

Magnetic tape

Magnetic tape provides only serial access. It can be referenced many times without the need for replacement. In addition, information can be erased by recording new information in its place. The tape has a ferromagnetic coating on a plastic base and is similar to the tape used on a tape recorder except that it is of a higher quality and more durable. The standard width is ½ in and it normally comes in reels of 2400 ft.

Information is retained on the tape in the form of magnetized and non-magnetized spots (representing 1s and 0s) which are arranged in tracks, normally nine, running the length of the tape (see figure 4.7). To represent a character in tracks, special codes are needed. Information recorded on magnetic tape is stored in varying densities, typically 1600 characters per inch (cpi) or even as dense as 6250 cpi, with the higher density applicable to the more modern and larger computer systems. The capacity of a tape depends on recording density, length of reel and proportion of tape that is actually used for recording.[13]

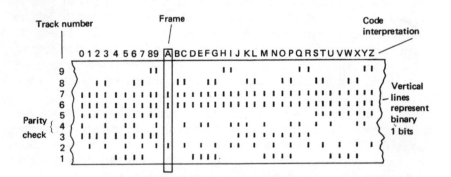

Figure 4.7 Nine-track magnetic tape. A parity bit is included on the tape for checking purposes. This figure illustrates a so-called odd parity tape on which all the frames contain an odd number of 1 bits. When a character is represented by an even number of 1 bits, a parity bit is added to make an odd number of 1 bits. When the data is transferred from the tape a check is made on the number of 1 bits, revealing an error if an even number is found

The traditional type of drive is depicted in figure 4.8. It can be seen that the tape runs from a supply reel to a pick-up reel via two vacuum channels and between a set of read/write heads. The two vacuum channels are designed to take up slack tape, acting as buffers to prevent the tape from snapping or stretching when starting from a stationary position or slowing down from full speed. The read/write heads are present either to access information, or to place information on the tape. They are a single unit, made up of one read/write head per track.

Another type of drive is the **cartridge tape drive**. It is small in comparison with the conventional drive often no bigger than a video recorder, and does not use the same vacuum feed principle. Tape of ¼ in width is used on some devices instead of the standard ½ in tape. Reels are normally shorter, typically 300 to 600 ft.

Even though information can only be accessed serially, magnetic tape is very widely used. Frequently it is necessary to copy information and to retain it in the same order for use on another occasion. Tape is ideal for this purpose as it is cheap and the transfer rate to and from the computer's main memory is relatively fast. A reel of tape is also a convenient way of carrying information from one place to another, i.e., transferring information between computer systems which are not linked together. Indeed, the programs provided by a computer manufacturer to help run a computer system are normally delivered to the customer on this medium. In addition, tape is widely used to

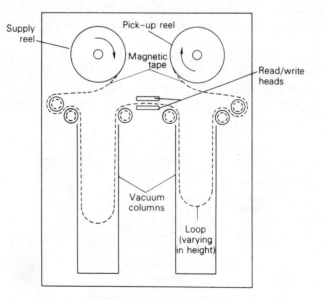

Figure 4.8 Typical magnetic tape drive

back-up information on magnetic disk (see figure 4.8). The use of cartridge tape for this purpose is associated particularly with microcomputer systems.

Besides acting as an area of secondary storage, magnetic tape is also an input/output medium in its own right. Information is input to the computer from the tape for processing and information is output to tape where it resides until it is needed again or until it becomes redundant and is erased.

Magnetic disk

This device allows direct access but can also be used in serial mode if required. In shape, a disk resembles an LP record. A disk pack consists of a number of these disks, six or more, mounted about half an inch apart on a central hub which rotates, spinning the disks at speeds of 60 or more revolutions a second. Information is recorded on both sides of each disk[14] as a series of magnetized or non-magnetized spots.

Information is stored on tracks arranged in concentric circles (figure 4.9), with each character represented by a pattern of bits in sequence on one track. Although varying in length, each track contains the same number of characters, which means that tracks on the outer reaches of the disk are less densely packed with characters than those towards the centre. Each track is normally subdivided into sectors and information is accessed by track and sector address (76;5, that is 76th track and 5th sector).

The diameter of a standard sized disk is 14 in and there may be several hundred tracks per surface (typically 400 to 1600) each with a storage capacity of thousands of characters. Disk packs are potentially very high capacity storage devices typically in the range 20 to 1000 megabytes (M bytes).[15]

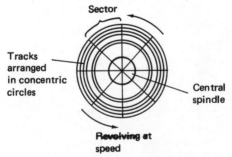

Figure 4.9 Tracks and sectors of a disk. There may be as many as 256 tracks and 32 or more sectors.

The disk pack on some disk storage devices is permanently fixed in position, whilst on others the pack can be removed and replaced by another in a matter of seconds. Not all disks are stacked in packs. A single removable disk is generally known as a cartridge disk. The facility to change packs or cartridges means that storage space can be increased without the heavy expense of buying another complete device.

There are two types of read/write head units for magnetic disk devices, a moving-head unit and a fixed-head unit (see figure 4.10). In the moving-head unit, the head moves horizontally across the surface of the disk so that it is able to access each track individually. There is a head for each surface and all the heads move in unison. Information stored on the tracks which constitute a cylindrical shape through the disk pack are therefore accessed simultaneously, a significant factor in storage arrangements. Exchangeable disk packs are only associated with moving-head units. In the case of the fixed-head unit, there is one read/write head for each track, as a result of which, no head movement is needed and information is therefore traced more quickly. The heads do not have direct contact with the surface but 'rest' on a cushion of air. The air movement caused by the revolving disk forces the head to 'fly' about 1/400th of an inch from the surface. However, dust particles can be a serious problem – even causing physical damage as well as data corruption.

The time taken to access information on these direct, or random, devices varies considerably, but the fixed-head device is quicker than the moving-head device.[16] As with magnetic tape, information on magnetic disk can be accessed again and again. When fresh data is recorded it simply replaces the existing information.

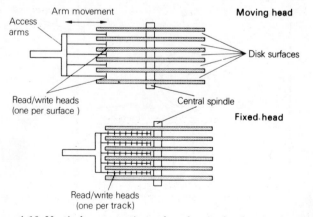

Figure 4.10 Vertical cross-sections of read-write head units for magnetic disk packs

Floppy disk

The floppy disk was developed in the early 1970s as a cheap and fast alternative to storage on magnetic tape. It is a small, random access disk which, like all secondary storage devices, can be used both for input and output operations. The disk is made of flexible plastic and coated in magnetic oxide. For protection, it is normally contained within a plastic or cardboard sleeve, often referred to as a cartridge (see figure 4.11). The cartridge is readily loaded into, and unloaded from, a drive unit. Unlike the moving-head read/write mechanism on conventional disk drives, the heads on a floppy disk unit make contact with the disk surface, when reading or writing, and disks therefore get worn with constant use.

There are two recognized standard sizes, 8 in and 5¼ in, frequently referred to as **diskette** and **mini-floppy** respectively. A more recent development is the 3½ in size.[17] Storage capacity is small compared with other conventional disk devices but quite impressive for size. The capacity of an 8 in diskette is typically between 250 K bytes and 1.5 M bytes and the capacity of a 5¼ in mini-floppy is between 125 K bytes and 500 K bytes, depending on density. The floppy disk is a low-cost device particularly suited to supporting personal computer systems and for use with small business and word processing systems.[18]

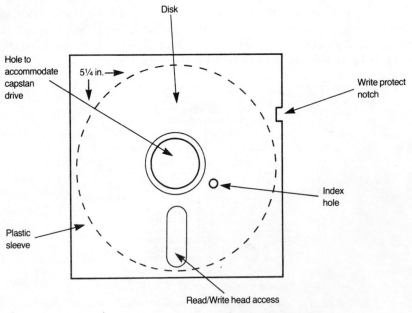

Figure 4.11 A floppy disk

Winchester disk

The most significant development in disk technology in recent years, in terms of realized potential, is the introduction of hermetically sealed units, generally known as Winchester disk drives, in which the read/write heads are designed to take off and land on the disk surface (see figure 4.12). The disk is coated with a special lubricant which reduces the friction when the heads land and the sealed chamber prevents contamination from dust and other airborne particles. The technology enables greater precision of alignment, an increase in the number of tracks on the disk surface and a higher storage density per track. Winchester disks are fast and highly reliable, yet low-priced compared with conventional hard disk devices. Because the units are sealed, preventative maintenance is not required. Disks are getting better all the time and research aimed at increasing capacity and reliability continues.

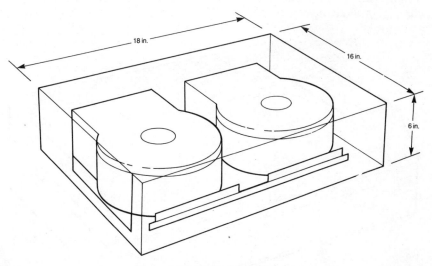

Figure 4.12 A Winchester disk drive

Standard sizes are 5 ¼ in, 8 in, and 14 in, but 8 in is the most common. Storage capacities range from around 10 Mb to 456 Mb (or even more). There are also 3 ½ in disks which can store 40 Mb or more. A magnetic tape cartridge system is often used to provide copies of information on disk for back up purposes and in a transportable magnetic tape form. Winchester disks are used to support minicomputers and microcomputers, and they compete with floppies in the rapidly expanding areas of personal computing, word processing and business applications.

Optical disk

The most exciting development in disk storage since the introduction of Winchester technology is that of CD-ROM (**compact disk read-only memory**). These are early days, but the impact is likely to be just as significant, for CD-ROM is able to provide enormous storage capacity for use with all manner of systems from huge mainframes to small desktop systems.

A single silvery plastic disk, or 'platter' as it is more commonly called, no more than 4.72 in in diameter is able to store up to 600 Mb of data. This is the equivalent of 1000 or more floppy disks or approximately 200,000 pages of text. CD-ROM uses the same metal-coated, plastic platters as used for digital audio recordings. The digital information is burned on in the same way by a laser. The playing surface is coated with a thin film of aluminium and this reflects the scanning laser beam of the CD-ROM player (or disk drive). A layer of clear resin covers the aluminium for protection. The CD-ROM player is essentially no more than an audio compact disk player.

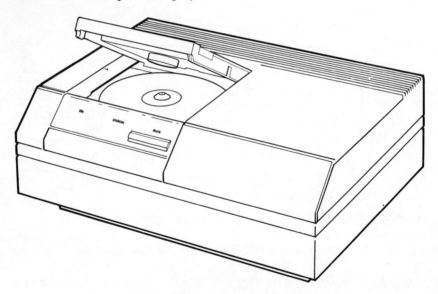

Figure 4.13 An optical disk drive

As the name suggests, information stored in CD-ROM can be read only. It cannot be modified in any way. CD-ROM is potentially useful for applications in which there is a database of information which is useful as it stands and does not need changing in any way, at least not over a reasonable period of time, e.g. a directory such as Yellow pages.

The drawbacks of CD-ROM are partially solved by the introduction of WORM (**write-once, read memory**). Here the information is permanent once it is placed in WORM but you do have the opportunity to place or update information, albeit once only. A third type, still very much under development, is the **erasable compact disk**. Once this type is thoroughly proven and accepted then the compact disk will be able to support applications in general.

Input direct to backing stores

In data processing where, traditionally, data preparation is a major part of the work, keying information directly to magnetic tape or disk is standard practice. Three methods are distinguishable:

- key-to-tape
- key-to-cassette/cartridge
- key-to-disk/diskette

When the information is eventually transferred from these backing stores, the backing stores themselves become 'input' devices.

Key-to-tape

A key-to-tape device, sometimes referred to as a magnetic tape encoder, permits the recording of information directly on magnetic tape. An operator, copying from documents, keys in the data which is stored temporarily by the device and typically displayed on a CRT for visual checking before being transferred to magnetic tape.

Key-to-cassette/cartridge

Information can also be keyed direct to small magnetic cassette tapes or cartridges and later transferred to standard magnetic tape for processing. A cassette, typically two and a half inches by four inches in size, is capable of storing around 200,000 characters of information. A typical cartridge is smaller in capacity, averaging around 30,000 characters. These key input devices are easy to use and compact, and are therefore most suitable for the collection of data at source, for example at places remote from the computer installation.

Key-to-disk/diskette

As with key-to-tape systems, information is entered via a keyboard and

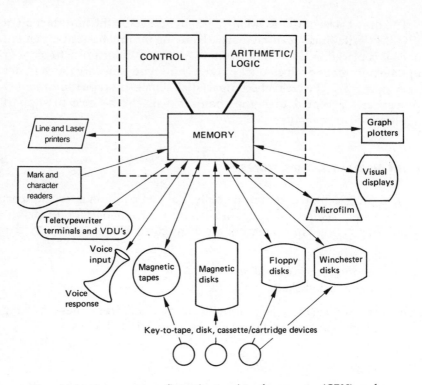

Figure 4.14 A computer configuration consists of a computer (CPU), and a number of peripheral devices. The work to be done at an installation determines which of the peripherals are required. It is not suggested that all the devices illustrated here will be found at any one installation

displayed on a CRT to allow a visual check. A key-to-disk/diskette system normally comprises a minicomputer, a number of key stations (one or more for a diskette system, typically 8 to 64 for a disk system) and a disk drive. The minicomputer is required to control the input from the various stations, enabling the data to be held temporarily for verification and editing before allocation to the disk store.

Backing stores serve two purposes. They supplement the internal memory of the computer when linked to the CPU, and they also store programs and data for **future** use. It is important to appreciate that information from backing stores has to pass into the internal memory (under the direction of control) before it can be used (see figure 4.14). This means that the CPU handles information from backing stores in much the same way as it handles information passing to and from conventional input/output devices.

NOTES

1 See Appendix One for descriptions of punched cards and paper tape.

2 Many devices both facilitate input and provide output. The VDU is one of these, and is described in the section on output (see page 51).

3 A terminal linked by telephone traditionally needs a device called a modem to convert the information into a form in which it can be transmitted. A second modem is required to reconvert it at the other end of the telephone link before the information is input to the computer. Advances in telecommunications have taken place which enable communication without the need for translation into analog signals. The change to digital communications is a significant step forward, and allows a much faster transfer rate.

4 Chapter Eight is entirely devoted to the subject of networks.

5 The dimensions of a compact, battery-driven microcomputer may be no bigger than 300 mm x 150 mm x 30 mm. Such a device may have a 48K ROM backed by 256K bytes of RAM, and an 8 line x 40 character LCD (liquid crystal display) screen with graphics capability.

6 Input of data direct to backing store is covered on page 65.

7 Typically, the whole line of information is transferred at one time by depressing a function key reserved for the purpose.

8 Desktop publishing (see page 112) is one example of an application enhanced by the use of a mouse. Under the control of the software and using special signs and symbols you can move and manipulate the pieces of text, together with graphics and diagrams, until you are entirely happy with the layout.

9 Limited graphics capability can be provided on video monitors attached to most microcomputers by adding so-called high resolution graphics boards to the micros.

10 In this context, a pixel is the smallest element of display.

11 There are devices which boast as many as 4096 different colours.

12 Some systems now use laser technology to produce print-out on microfilm.

13 Information is not stored continuously but in blocks of a fixed length with gaps (inter-record gaps) in between. Typically the capacity of a 2400 ft tape at 1600 and 6250 bpi is 40 and 140 Mbs respectively.

14 Except often, the outer side of the top and bottom of the pack.

15 1 megabyte = 1 million bytes. Typically, one character can be stored per byte and thus an 80 megabyte (Mb) disk has the capacity to store 80 million characters. A full page of this text comprises some 3200 characters and at this rate, the disk could retain 25,000 pages.

16 Seek and access times are very fast, measured in microseconds (ms) e.g., 30ms (1ms = 1 millionth of a second).

17 Some manufacturers have opted for 3¼ in rather than 3½ in. As yet there is no industry standard, but most recognize 3 ½ in.

18 See Chapter Nine.

5
Computer Languages

In the previous chapter, we looked at machine/human communication devices. In this chapter and the next, we turn our attention to how man instructs a computer to perform given tasks or applications.

Humans communicate with each other through languages such as English, Italian, and so forth. They are highly developed so that we can express not only facts but also abstract ideas, as well as conveying shades of meaning or suggesting subtle feelings and sensations. But, in order to do so, a large vocabulary is required. In contrast, the 'natural' language of the computer is far less exotic and has a comparatively restricted vocabulary. We shall see why in the next chapter.

People can use natural languages *incorrectly* and still make themselves understood. Computers, however, are not yet able to correct and deduce meaning from incorrect instructions. Computer languages are smaller and simpler than natural languages but they have to be used with far greater precision. Unless a programmer adheres *exactly* to the 'grammar' of a programming language, even down to the correct punctuation, the computer will be unable to execute the instructions.

In this chapter we look at the two main levels of computer languages, the so-called *high* and *low* levels and then, in Chapter Six, discuss some of the basic principles underlying programming.

TYPES OF LANGUAGES

Three types of computer languages have evolved over the years:

- machine code
- assembly code
- high level code.

It should be appreciated that of the three, the only type which the computer itself can understand is machine code. The other two are 'variations' of machine code but are orientated more towards the human programmer than the computer itself. Machine code is at the binary level, that is, it consists of patterns of binary digits. Each make of computer is designed to recognize only one machine code so that a machine code designed for computer X would be totally unrecognized by computer Y. Both machine code and assembly code are called **low level languages** as opposed to the third which is a **high level language.** We shall discuss the three types briefly so that we can appreciate the meaning of the terms high and low levels.

Machine codes

To understand the structure of a machine code, there are two facts discussed in Chapter Two which we need to recall. The first, is that a machine instruction has a two-part format, as in figure 5.1.

OPERATION (Code)	ADDRESS (Location)

Figure 5.1

The second point is that both parts are represented internally in the machine's store as a string of binary digits. It should be no surprise, therefore, that some of the first programmers (those, for example, who worked on the Manchester Mark 1 described in Appendix One) actually wrote their instructions in binary. However, since human programmers are more familiar with the decimal system, most of them preferred to write the two-part instructions in decimal, and leave the input device to convert these into binary. The set of instruction codes (whether in binary or decimal) created in conjunction with the computer designer, is called a **machine code** or **machine language.** It will be determined by certain design features of the computer itself, e.g. the type of registers and the number of bits (word length) each register can hold in the CPU; the word length of the memory unit; etc. Matters become more complex here because some computers have variable word lengths and others have no word length as such but merely a succession of bit places. Clearly, because of this dependence of the language upon a particular computer's architecture, such machine code languages are called machine-dependent or machine-orientated languages.

Assembly codes

The numeric machine codes (decimal or binary) are often difficult to remember and, even with a code book or glossary, encoding is a laborious process and mistakes can be made easily. To overcome these problems, the idea of mnemonics (or memory aids) was introduced. The human mind can more easily identify with mnemonics or abbreviated words than a series of digits, for example, a computer may be designed to interpret the machine code 1001 (binary) or 09 (decimal) as the operation 'multiply', but it is easier for the human being to remember it as MULT or MLT.

A repertoire of codes evolved, therefore, using readily identifiable mnemonics, e.g., DIV (divide), SUB (subtract), etc. Although this made life easier for the programmer, it made things more involved for the computer.

The MLT has to be translated into the binary pattern '1001' before the machine can 'understand' the operation intended. The act of translating is carried out by a special pre-stored program called an **assembler**. It translates the program written by the programmer into that version which the machine recognizes and responds to, and 'assembles' it in the main memory ready for execution, hence the term **assembly codes.**

Machine and assembly codes, being orientated towards the basic design of computers, are referred to as 'low-level' languages.

High-level languages

The commercial viability and wider use of computers led, by the mid-1950s, to the necessity for, and development of, 'high-level' languages.

These languages, instead of being machine based, are orientated more towards the problem to be solved. Such problem-orientated languages enable the programmer to write instructions using certain English words and conventional mathematical notations, therefore making it easier for the programmer to think about the problem. This means that the two-part format of a low-level instruction (operation code/location address) is no longer necessary in a high-level instruction. As an example, we give a high-level instruction (in FORTRAN – see Appendix Two) to 'multiply two numbers together and add a third number to their sum'. The familiar algebraic notation for this is: $x = a \times b + c$.

FORTRAN, being orientated towards the solution of mathematical problems, allows the programmer a similar ease in describing the same instruction, thus: $X = A * B + C$.

The only differences between the two forms are FORTRAN's use of capital letters and an asterisk in place of the more familiar multiplication symbol.

Translation stage

By using high level languages, the programmer saves a great deal of time and effort. To describe the above mathematical expression in a low level language would involve a minimum of five separate instructions instead of the one shown. Furthermore, high level languages can be used on almost any computer so that a program written for one machine could be executed on another with minor alterations. This portability is one of the major reasons for using high level languages. This seems to contradict the earlier statement that a computer can recognize but one language, the one specially designed for it. No computer can recognize a high level code until it has been translated into the machine code of the computer. This is rather like my inability to converse in Chinese. What I require is a human translator to translate my English into Chinese and vice versa so that I can hold an effective conversation.

Computers, therefore, need to have a high level language program translated into machine code before it can be understood and obeyed. This translation stage is carried out by a specially written (and costly) program. Depending on the high level language in use, the translator may be a **compiler** or an **interpreter.** These programs may be pre-stored in ROM or kept on some form of mass storage such as a magnetic disk. Figure 5.2 illustrates this process. The programmer's code in high level

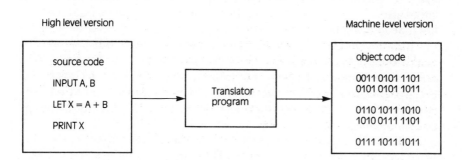

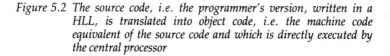

Figure 5.2 The source code, i.e. the programmer's version, written in a HLL, is translated into object code, i.e. the machine code equivalent of the source code and which is directly executed by the central processor

language *X* is called the **source code.** The translator will convert this into machine code the result being called the **object code.** Both the source and the object codes are the same program, but in different formats. The first is more easily written by the human, the other is in a state which the computer itself can understand and execute.

A FORTRAN compiler can only translate source code written in FORTRAN and, therefore, a translator is required for each high level language supported by a given computer system. Furthermore, since the object code is generated for one particular machine, each make of computer will require its individual compiler. The same applies to interpreters.

Compilers versus interpreters

Compilers convert or *translate* the *entire* source program into object code before the program is executed. Interpreters, on the other hand, translate one source instruction into object code and the computer immediately executes that instruction before moving on to translate the next instruction. This means that some instructions, such as repeated loops may be re-interpreted time and again. Interpreted programs tend to take longer to complete execution than compiled programs. However, an advantage of the interpreter is that if an error is made in a given instruction, the programmer knows exactly at which point the error occurred.

High versus low level languages

We have considered the three types of programming languages. In most cases, programmers mainly work in a high-level language, but low-level languages are still used by those programmers who need to work at machine level. There are many high-level languages, but they can be grouped into four broad application areas; scientific, business, special purpose and interactive (see Appendix Two). The language chosen will be largely determined by two factors: the application in hand and the choice offered by the computer installation, i.e., the range of language translators which are available.

High level languages have the following advantages: they are easier to learn, to understand and to write. They are certainly easier to correct and, in general, they are portable. Low level languages require far less space in memory, execute more quickly and permit the programmer to have more control over the internal workings of the computer. On the other hand, they are more difficult to learn and use, since the programmer requires quite extensive knowledge of the machine's architecture.

OTHER LANGUAGES

The so-called high level languages such as FORTRAN, COBOL, PASCAL, etc. are known as third generation languages. Higher levels exist such as software packages and fourth generation languages (4GLs). A software package is simply a program complete with user documentation, i.e., a manual which explains how to use the program. Today, many people make use of word processing, data base and spreadsheet packages as well as graphics packages (see page 132). These are sometimes integrated into one complete suite. The user of such programs need know nothing about programming or even about computers to be able to use them successfully. It was their availability for the micro that has projected these programs into everyday use.

Fourth generation languages are something quite different. It is difficult to give a definition since there are many 4GLs available, suited to a whole range of tasks. Some require considerable programming expertise, others require experience of **systems analysis;** some are designed to run on a variety of computers, others restricted to a particular model; some try to provide a variety of functions within a given organization, others restrict their applications to specific areas of the computerized organization. A simple way to appreciate 4GLs is to view them as consisting of a set of tools, like that possessed by a carpenter. One or more of the tools are selected as and when they are required, each being designed to cope with a specific task. In general, these languages are for the more experienced computer personnel.

Although third generation languages can do all that fourth generation languages can do (and have done so for decades), it became evident that, with the increased demands on data processing departments, more and more applications were taking longer and longer to complete. In an attempt to improve productivity in DP departments, 4GLs were introduced. At the time of writing, there is a distinct division of opinion as to how successful they really are. Some claim that life began to be worthwhile again after using 4GLs; others claim that life, not good before, has been made worse since climbing onto the 4GL bandwagon. Time will tell.

STEPS IN PROGRAM DEVELOPMENT

There are two broad categories of programmer, the successful and the not-so-successful. Upon being given a problem to solve, the latter category rush to their keyboards and begin coding, i.e. the actual writing of instructions. It is the mark of professional and successful programmers that this is one of the last stages they undertake. There are many more important steps to consider first. It is not possible to study programming in any depth in this text, but we shall look at some of the stages involved in writing a program in the hope that should you ever need to write a program you will at least be aware of the total process.

If you adopt the stages set out below, not only are you more likely to end up with a program that works but you will do so in a fraction of the time that you would have spent otherwise. The amateur never believes this and wonders why so much time is spent correcting (de-bugging) programs. This is summed up in one of the well-known proverbs which circulate amongst the programming fraternity:

The sooner you begin to code, the longer it takes.

Understand the problem

Unless the problem is clearly understood, you cannot even begin to solve it. This seems like a truism until you appreciate that a program specification seldom gives all the facts required by the programmer. The professional programmer is a pessimist, because from past experience there is always some important information which is omitted. This needs to be identified first.

Examine the data

Programs are written to work on data. Unless one knows exactly how the data is organized, what it 'looks' like, etc., the program which processes it cannot be written. This fact becomes clearer the more one writes programs, but it is a fact all too frequently overlooked by the novice.

Plan the output

The output should be planned next. Not only does this help to ensure that nothing is omitted from the program, but it helps to get a clear picture of what the program is trying to achieve and whether the programmer really does understand the problem.

Designing the solution

There are many ways of designing solutions, so much so that entire books are devoted to this subject alone. Computer scientists frequently say that programming is like any engineering task in that the program has to be designed and constructed in much the same way as any engineering project. A motorway is not built by starting at point A and steadfastly pushing onto point X. Rather, months are spent in planning; charts designed; sub-tasks identified as well as those which cannot begin until others have been completed; broad designs are developed and later more detailed designs constructed. It is only after a long planning period and the most effective order of the sub-tasks is agreed upon that the construction crews actually begin work. Programming requires this same painstaking process, with the end result standing or falling by the amount of care and attention invested in the planning stage.

Selecting test data

How can one ensure that once a program is eventually working the results it produces are 'correct'? The answer is simple common sense. Try the program out on some data to which the answers have been worked out in advance. If they match, the program should be all right. Selecting effective test data is a serious exercise and the more significant the program, the more care needs to be taken in the selection.

The actual coding

At this stage, one can begin to code the detailed program designs into program instructions of a given language. If all the previous steps have been completed with due diligence, this coding should be almost 'automatic'. The chances are high that a fairly successful program will result first time around. Although it may still contain bugs (errors), these should be fewer and relatively easy to identify and correct.

Testing

The program can be tested with the test data, results checked and any errors amended. When all is correct, the program can be released and set to work on live data.

The above steps are a gross simplification of what is involved in the preparation of significant programs. Teams of experts will be brought in at one or more of the various stages; months of work and much money invested. The whole art of programming requires practice, years of experience and a thorough study of programming methodology. We introduce some of the basic concepts of programming methodology in the next chapter.

6

Principles of Programming

In this chapter, we shall look at some of the basic principles behind programming and introduce the concepts of structured programming. The reader should be aware that the aim of this chapter is to provide an insight to these subjects and that those intending to take programming seriously will require a more formal treatment.

SIX FUNDAMENTAL CONCEPTS

We begin by looking at six fundamental and somewhat obvious concepts. These are obvious to the experienced programmer, of course, but are surprisingly opaque to those new to the art of programming and can form a hurdle until appreciated.

1. Programs are created *solely* to work on data; without data a program has nothing to work on and would not need to be written in the first place.

2. Programs lie *inside* the CPU, data lies *outside*. Consequently, it is the program which must call in data when required (via input operations); the program must also perform output operations so that the results of processing the data are visible to the human being in the outside world.

3. Data, then, becomes a major consideration for any programmer, perhaps even more important than the choice of programming language. The programmer needs to know exact details about the format of the data itself. It is only through experience that the truth of this statement becomes apparent.

4 Programs are written to have a general nature. No-one should consider writing a program to process one set of data otherwise, once the program is executed and the results produced, it is never required again. Programs are written in a generalized manner to perform the same set of operations time and again but on a whole range of given data sets.

5 Once the control unit begins to execute a program, it starts with the first instruction and continues to execute each instruction in turn, one after the other. The only time it will not execute the next instruction in sequence is when the program specifically tells the control unit to execute an instruction at some other point in a program. This is known as the **logic** of the program and the conscious action by the programmer is known as transferring control.

6 Many people, new to programming bring a preconceived idea that programming is a complicated and difficult art. They tend to think that unless they adopt 'clever' programming techniques, the computer will somehow 'look down' on their efforts. Now this is far from the truth. And the most important principle for any programmer to adhere to is to keep *simple!*

COMPUTER OPERATIONS

From the previous chapters, we can conclude that in the final analysis, computers are capable of performing only four basic operations:

- input and output operations
- arithmetic and logical operations
- movement of data within the CPU
- primitive comparison/logic operations

Input operations are necessary simply to allow the internal world of the CPU to react to external stimulus either from sensors of some kind or from the human being entering data at a keyboard. Having processed results, the user needs to see the output.

Arithmetic and logical operations are performed in the ALU.

Movement of data is required to transfer data from one unit, perform processes on the data and to transfer the results back into central memory.

Comparison/logic operations are less easy to describe without direct reference to programming. It simply means that two values (either numbers or characters, such as two names) are compared for equality or to find if one is greater/smaller than the other and, depending upon the outcome, the control unit will execute one of two possible instructions which will be in different places in a program. In this way, a programmer may decide which of two courses of action to pursue. For this reason, this kind of operation is often referred to as a decision-making process. It is very simple and herein lies the problem. Too many simple comparison/logic operations create too many logic paths through the program so that one ends up with a spaghetti-like program (see figure 6.1). It then becomes all too easy to make errors by moving to the wrong instruction.

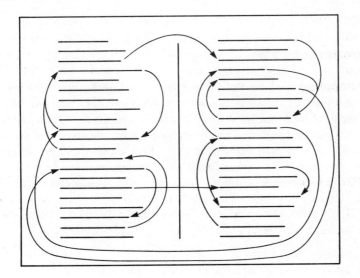

Figure 6.1 The 'spaghetti bowl' program

When one realizes that a problem has to be decomposed into only four primitive operations, the novice might well be forgiven if he/she wonders what all the fuss is about. Surely, it must be quite simple! This is true: programming in high level languages is not a complicated affair when one considers the operations performed. But this is exactly where the problems occur. Any significant programming task using these simple units must result in a long and complex program. The logic (where the next instruction to be executed lies) becomes confused, bugs abound and de-bugging becomes a tedious procedure.

This was pointed out by Dijkstra in 1968 and, furthermore, he identified the root cause, the GOTO, hence the title of his famous letter. This resulted in the birth of the so-called Structured Programming movement. The actual term structured programming dates from the publication of a book by that title in 1972. Since then, the term has become widely used and, depending upon context, has different meanings. For our purpose, I borrow from Schneider *et al* (see References):

> Although structured programming does not yet have a fixed definition, its most important concerns are for the types of control statements needed in a programming language and the relationship between certain control structures and a program's clarity.

It remains for us to examine what these authors mean by control statements and control structures and why these are needed.

PROGRAM PROCESSES

It has been proved by Bohm and Jacopini (see References) that three structures are all that are needed to solve any logic problem. These are sequence, choice and repetition. It can be shown that each part of any program can be converted to one or more of these three basic structures. (Figures 6.2, 6.3 and 6.4 illustrate these.) Although these are sufficient to code any computer problem, additional structures have been defined to add to programmer convenience yet without detracting from the original theory (see figures 6.5 and 6.6).

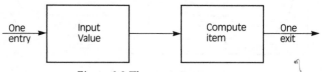

Figure 6.2 The sequence process

STRUCTURED PROGRAMMING

It is too simple to say that structured programming is one which contains few (or no) GOTOs. However, this lies at the heart of the matter. The simple comparison/logic operation which the computer performs forces the programmer to make undue use of the GOTO instruction and, according to Dijkstra, results in programming errors. Therefore, certain structures were devised which would help to

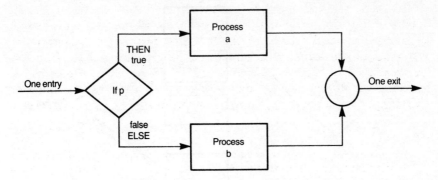

Figure 6.3 The choice process: IFTHENELSE

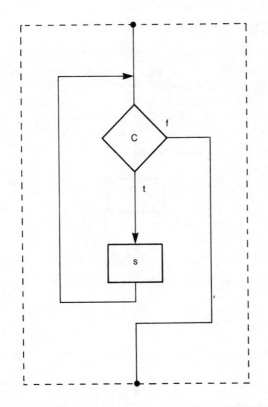

Figure 6.4 The repetition process using the DOWHILE

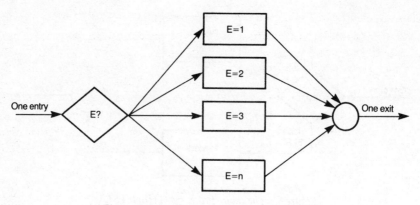

Figure 6.5 Another choice process using CASE

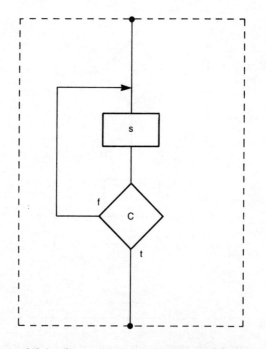

Figure 6.6 Another repetition process using REPEATUNTIL

eliminate the use of the GOTO and at the same time make the program far more readable. In addition, those familiar with these structures could amend (maintain) programs more effectively.

The essential choice structure is shown in Figure 6.3: the IFTHENELSE construction. CASE is an additional choice structure which proves to be more convenient in certain circumstances without detracting from the structure of a program. Likewise, Figure 6.4 illustrates the DOWHILE structure for repetition. The REPEATUNTIL construct being an additional feature which can be more appropriate in some situations.

And there we have the programmer's whole bag of tricks. What, then, makes programming so difficult? The actual coding of instructions should be an almost automatic procedure presenting an experienced programmer with few problems, provided that all the steps which precede this stage have been carried out meticulously. These were discussed in Chapter Five and encompass the art of systems analysis. It is this aspect which really makes or breaks a computerized application. It includes those four steps mentioned in the previous chapter and which are discussed further in Chapter Ten.

7

Introduction to Computer and Operating Systems

Few people today communicate *directly* with a computer. Instead, they communicate with a computer via an **operating system.** The more 'friendly' the operating system, the easier it is for people to interface with and make use of the computer. In the past, computer users tended to be specialists who were quite willing to spend a great deal of time and effort in learning how to communicate with their computer. Today, with the proliferation of computer users, due in no small measure to the microcomputer, the demand for more 'friendly' and easy to use interface systems is increasing.

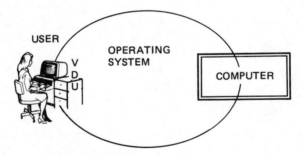

Figure 7.1 The operating system acts as an 'interface' between the USER and the COMPUTER

Although we talk about *an* operating system, it is really a collection of separate units (programs) which function as a harmonious whole, for example:

- the *language translators* – which convert source code into machine code;
- the *disk operating system* – which transfers data and programs to and from the disk into and out of central memory;

84

- the *text editor* – a program which allows a user to correct or amend any information stored on disk/tape; to add new information or to remove (delete) unwanted information;
- *direct commands to save, rename, copy, delete and print* files of data or programs or list the names of files held on mass storage.

Today there are many types of computer systems, e.g., batch processing, time-sharing, real-time, multi-tasking, multi-user, stand-alone systems. An operating system must take account of the type of computer system in use as well as providing the user with the facilities mentioned above. In this chapter, we shall examine briefly these systems, in roughly the order of their historical development. For many topics in computing, it is best to ignore the past and to jump straight into current technology and methods. However, an historical perspective, even to the extent of discussing punched cards (the most widely used input medium for several decades), greatly aids an appreciation of current trends. Of necessity, we mention these systems in relation to mainframe and mini-computers but the same principles stand when applied to microcomputers.

EARLY COMPUTER CONFIGURATIONS

In the early days of computing, if one had a problem for computer solution one first had to build a computer. SEAC is an example of a machine especially built for the particular needs of the National Bureau of Standards. The designers of such computers, or their close associates, also programmed the solution, and in many cases, performed all the necessary duties which an operator would perform today (feeding cards to the card reader, paper to the printer, manipulating switches etc.). They had an intimate knowledge of their machine and could follow the progress of a program via the pattern of lights displayed on the control panel(s), known as the *console*, which showed the instruction currently being executed, the addresses involved, the contents of registers (the accumulator, for example), and so forth. When the program was completed, the programmer left the machine free for the next person.

The configuration (hardware) then in use was simple, as figure 7.2 suggests. There was an input device (card reader or paper tape reader), the central processing unit, an output device (usually, a printer), and a console which allowed instructions to be directly keyed into the CPU, and which also displayed the calculations or data manipulations which were taking place inside the CPU.

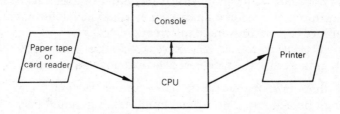

Figure 7.2 A simple configuration

Programmers today do not have the same intimacy with their machines as their predecessors. The change in relationship has come about because of the increasing differences which soon evolved between the awesome speeds of processors and the relatively slow peripheral devices.

Peripheral and CPU speeds

Card readers operate at speeds between 100 and 2000 cards per minute. For an 80-column card, this is:

100 x 80 x 1/60 = approx. 133 characters per second (cps)
2000 x 80 x 1/60 = approx. 2666 cps.

Line printers can print at rates in excess of 2000 characters per second. Such speeds may well be impressive particularly when compared to human typists. However, they are nothing compared to the internal electronic speeds of the CPU. Working at the speed of electricity, approximately that of light, namely, 186,000 miles per second, or 982,000,000 feet per second, some ten million characters can be transferred internally, or three million calculations computed, within the space of one second, in the case of some of the faster mainframe computers.

In other words, while a card reader is supplying just one character to the main store, the CPU can perform many thousands of internal operations before it needs to become involved with the next character from the card reader. I/O (input/output) operations are considerably slower compared to the internal operations of the CPU. It was the attempt to overcome this speed mis-match which led to the introduction of computer systems. This situation was not so acute with the early, slower computers. But, as internal processing speeds increased, as well as the number of programs to be processed, the method whereby one programmer loaded his own cards and operated the machine himself could only lead to serious misuse of computing power. Clearly, some means of accelerating the I/O phases was required.

The first significant attempt came with the development of magnetic tape. Now cards could first be read via the card reader, and the information copied onto a magnetic tape. From this tape, information could then be passed to the processor at speeds between 20,000 and 300,000 cps. Likewise, results produced during processing could be transferred at this faster rate to a tape which, in turn, could then be output via the line printer. System programs, such as assemblers, could also be kept on magnetic tape instead of having to be read via the card reader each time they were used. The stage was now set for the introduction of batch processing.

MAINFRAME OPERATING SYSTEMS

Batch processing

With the increase in the number of programs to be run, it made more sense to collect several at a time (a batch), and read them onto the input tape to form, in effect, a queue of programs. As the central processor completed one program, there was another waiting on the input tape.

In this way, the main processor was not held up by the slower speeds of card readers or line printers but could work at the full speed of the magnetic tape, and, later, disks. Batch processing was an improvement over the single-job submission and frequently increased the number of programs executed by 50 per cent or more.

Multi-programming

With batch processing, programs are called in sequence one at a time into the central memory for processing. When there is only one program in main memory, two of the CPU's most significant features may be underutilized, its expensive memory and the full capabilities of the ALU. Not every program will be large enough to fill the central memory. Not every program will be purely computational. The large commercial type of program normally reads in vast amounts of data, performs very little computation and outputs large amounts of information. We call these programs *I/O bound*, since the majority of work they perform is input–output.

The answer is to use a multi-programming system which enables more than one program to reside in central memory at the same time, so that when program A is reading in data or outputting results (I/O operations), program B's instructions can be executed (performed). If both programs are involved in I/O activity, then program C can be executed. The actual number of programs allowed in store at any given time will vary depending upon the operating system in use at a particular installation. Those jobs awaiting entry into the central memory are formed into a queue on a fast secondary storage device such as a magnetic disk.

For multi-programming to work satisfactorily, large memories are required (of the order of 128K), together with fast secondary storage devices and fast ALUs. Only the computer itself is capable of switching the CPU from one program to another fast enough. Hence, this task must be incorporated into the overall operating system, usually called the *supervisor*, but given different names by different manufacturers. For example, IBM call it the *monitor* and ICL, the *executive*.

Its main duty is to monitor the activity of the program currently being executed, so that at the appropriate time, it can switch control to another program, and control the flow of programs into the main memory from the entry queue. If must also keep all the results for the various programs in separate areas. This is achieved by allotting each program a separate space on magnetic disk (forming, in effect, a results queue ready for output). If you think back to the discussion on serial and direct access methods, it should be clear that a direct access storage device is needed for this results queue. The use of serial magnetic tape would not be a good way of achieving this. (It is possible, but the tapes would have to be continually rewound, thus reducing the efficiency of this method.)

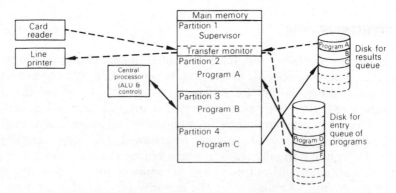

Figure 7.3 Memory partitioning in multi-programming

Figure 7.3 illustrates the principle of a multi-programming system: The main memory is divided into sections or partitions. The first partition is reserved for the supervisor, which has to remain in main memory all the time. The other three partitions (in this instance) each hold a program, A, B and C. Although there are more than two programs in main memory, only *one* is ever being executed at any point in time. Program B is currently being executed and Program C is passing some results to disk. Program A has completed its work and is being replaced by Program D from the entry queue. Note that a second disk is illustrated to hold the results of each program in separate areas.

A part of the supervisor partition is reserved permanently to organize the transfer of these queued results from the disk to the line printer. This we shall call a transfer monitor. It is also used to build up the entry queue on disk, which has been input from a card reader (Program F in the diagram).

When a job is submitted for processing, some time will elapse before the output is available. The length of time involved, called the **turn-around time,** will depend upon the number and size of jobs ahead of you. For some applications time is critical. Results may be needed in seconds rather than in hours. Time-sharing systems make this possible.

Time-sharing

Users of a time-sharing system communicate with their computer via a visual display terminal which is connected to the computer by land or telephone lines. In this way, they have a direct means of communicating with the central processor. Time-sharing systems have many, even hundreds, of terminals linked up to the central processor at the same time. However, if time-sharing is to be effective each user will require a response to a query from the computer within two to five seconds. We shall now explore that aspect of such systems which allows many users to be given this fast response.

The strategy of a time-sharing supervisor (resident in main memory all the time) is different from that of a multi-programming supervisor. The CPU can still only execute one program at a time and, clearly, the concept of one, possibly lengthy, program being completed before another one can be allowed into main memory from the input queue cannot apply here, otherwise certain users are going to have to wait for more than a few seconds before they can execute their programs. The basic idea behind time-sharing systems is to allow *all* programs to have a brief share of the central processor in turn. The time-sharing supervisor gives each job a short period of time during which it is in sole control of the processor. This short period of time is known as a *time slice, time slot* or *quantum*, typically 10 milliseconds.

If there are, let us say, ten terminals in use, user 1 is allowed to have his program executed and when his time period expires, or if his program becomes involved in an input–output request (thereby not requiring the central processor), the supervisor schedules the processor for user 2. User 1's program is swapped out of memory and user 3 swapped in. During this time, user 2 has control of the central processor. This swapping process, sometimes known as *roll-in roll-out*, is repeated many times within a few seconds. Thus, when a user's job is being executed it is in main store, but when it is not being executed it will be on secondary storage. Disks are the only feasible secondary storage devices since they have a much faster rate of information transfer than magnetic tape and provide direct access.

When it is realized that some computers can perform 3 million calculations in one second, but that experienced terminal users can only input information at whatever speed they can type, and are often engaged in comparatively long thinking spells, then it can be appreciated that modern time-sharing systems can service many terminals in the space of one second.

In time-sharing systems, a transfer monitor is required to co-ordinate the flow of information between the terminals and the disk storage. It is resident in the central memory and works in conjunction with the time-sharing supervisor which is responsible for the overall operation of the time-sharing system. Figure 7.4 illustrates these concepts and shows Terminal 1's program being swapped out, Terminal N's program being swapped in, whilst Terminal 2's program is currently being executed.

Real-time processing

The expression 'real-time' is applied to any system which produces an almost immediate response as a result of inputting data. The essential feature is that the input data must be processed quickly enough *so that further action can then be promptly taken on the results.*

Two examples of systems which operate in real-time are process control systems (as in nuclear reactor plants and steel mills) and transaction systems (such as airline reservations).

In a process control situation, one set of results may be used as essential data for the next stage of the process. The time interval between processing one set of data, and providing the results for the next input phase, may be as little as a few microseconds. Whatever the time interval, it is important that it is not exceeded.

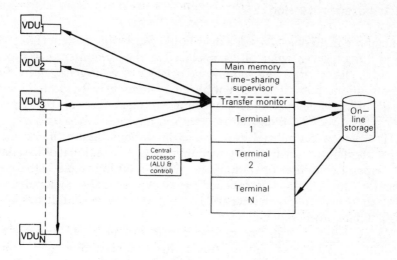

Figure 7.4 Concept of a time-sharing system

In the case of transaction systems, the period may be extended to a few seconds or even minutes, rather than microseconds. But the point to note is that once a particular transaction has been processed (reserving for Mr X a seat on the 9.30 a.m. flight from Heathrow to Rome), the files need to be updated before the next transaction can be processed. Real-time systems cannot break down without causing some disruption. This is one difference between real-time and time-sharing; the latter *should* not fail, but if it does the outcome is never disastrous. In many instances, real-time systems are duplicated so that, in the event of a break down, back-up facilities are immediately available. This makes these systems very expensive but, in the environments to which they are applied, a fail-safe system is essential.

Computer networks

A logical extension of time-sharing systems enables users to have access to more than one computer installation in order to share some computer facility or stored information peculiar to one centre. The various sites are connected via some form of communications network, such as the public telephone service, satellites or private lines. This linking together of distinct installations is called a *computer network system* and forms the subject of Chapter Eight.

Distributed processing

One of the main objectives of a distributed processing system is to place computing power where it is needed, in the computer user's own locality. Historically, and mainly for reasons of economics, individual organizations possess large centralized systems usually located at the head office. Regional offices wishing to make use of the central computer do so on a time-sharing, multi-programming basis.

However, a centralized system has limitations; firstly, if the main computer fails to function (not uncommon) then all regional offices have to suspend computer operations, resulting in an inevitable bottle-neck once the main system is functioning again; secondly, regional users have to format their own data at the direction of some central and often distant data processing manager.

Today, there is an increasing desire to get away from these limitations. The possibility of doing this has been due in no small measure to the growing use of low cost mini and micro systems being installed at local sites. Each local centre can now process on site much of its day-to-day work and thus have direct control over its own equipment as well as its own data formats, and, if necessary, possess hardware which exactly suits its own particular requirements. (Local control will not, of course, eliminate all problems.) But this is merely a decentralized system. To have a distributed processing system it is necessary for all the local centres to be linked together in a network so, should one site have a computing task which the local centre cannot process by itself, then that centre can 'call upon' additional assistance from one or more of the other sites. Thus the main characteristic of a distributed system is one in which a user's task, on a given occasion, can be divided up and distributed across a number of computer installations.

A user in a distributed system should confidently expect that *most* of his work can be dealt with adequately by his own installation; indeed, his own site is specifically designed to perform the majority of tasks. It is only in the *exceptional* circumstances that he needs to rely on the transmission of his task to the other sites.

MICROCOMPUTER OPERATING SYSTEMS

At the heart of every computer, large and small, lies the CPU. It is this unit which controls the operation of the other units attached to the system such as input, output and mass storage devices. All computers have a 'control program' to oversee this activity. Over the years, the term **operating system** has been in common use to refer to this control program. Mainframe and minicomputers have their own operating system and users require special training in order to communicate with such systems.

Users of microcomputers require some form of operating system as well. One of the earliest and most common was the Control Program for Microcomputers (CP/M). Its design was based around a specific medium, namely, the floppy disk, and in reality it was a disk operating system (DOS). CP/M was only a 'single user' or stand-alone operating system, i.e., it could handle the execution of only one program or task at a time.

As the popularity of microcomputers increased so have the demands of the users. Some require multiuser (more than one user at a time) and multi-tasking (the ability of the user to run more than one program at a time) capabilities. To meet these demands, an MP/M operating system, based on CP/M, was developed.

CP/M was originally based on the Intel 8080 microprocessor which, in 1973, was the first device powerful enough to be used in a microcomputer. Since that time, other 8-bit processors have been introduced such as the Intel 8085 and the highly popular Zilog Z80 chip. These compatible microprocessors also supported CP/M.

Although these microprocessors are still used, technological advances have led to 16-bit processor chips such as the Intel 8086 and 8088, the Motorola 68000, the Zilog Z8000 and the National Semiconductor 16000. 32-bit chips are becoming increasingly used such as Zilog's iAPX-432, Motorola's MC68020 and Intel's 80386. Other operating systems, then, are needed to interface these microprocessors to peripheral and storage devices.

CP/M-86 and MP/M-86 are the 16-bit counterparts to the CP/M and MP/M. MS-DOS was developed to run with the Intel's 8088 chip. IBM entered the microcomputer world and developed its own version of MS-DOS calling it PC-DOS. Because of the influence of IBM, many micro manufacturers tend to make their machines compatible with the IBM machines so that MS-DOS is perhaps the most common operating system for a whole range of microcomputers. One great advantage of this is that any package written to run under MS-DOS is able to be used on a variety of different machines which use that operating system. This helped to make the word processing package, WordStar, and the data base management package, dBASE, two of the most widely used programs on micros.

Another popular operating system is UNIX; originally developed independently of any machine or manufacturer. Its origins go back to 1969 and pre-date microcomputers. It was already established when the

16- and 32-bit processors were developed so that the increase in their use has led to a similar increase in the use of UNIX. However, at the time of writing, there is no one dominant operating system in use on 32-bit micros.

SUMMARY

In this chapter we have indicated that the average computer user does not usually deal directly with a computer, but with a computer system, via an operating system. Our contact with a computer complex may be through a small computer, a VDU or teletypewriter terminal. However, the CPU at the heart of the installation is surrounded by layers of software. We must not lose sight of the fact that, no matter how complex an operating system may appear, all that is happening at the heart of the machine is the interplay between the four basic operations of input–output, arithmetic, logical and comparison operations, and internal movement of information within the CPU. It may be that the program is simple, adding two numbers and outputting the result; it may be the final sales statistics which lead to a mammoth take-over bid; it may be the calculation of the strength of a heart beat whereby the means of saving a patient's life can be determined. To the basic machine, none of this matters. It performs its four operations 'mindlessly', untouched by the effect of the results. It is the intricate web of software surrounding the basic machine which makes it possible for the program to provide the great variety of information which *is* of human importance.

8

Computer Networks

As the volume of information in most fields of interest grows, so issues of information dissemination and access become more significant. Networking holds the key to this by providing the means to exchange information and to share the resources involved. A network can link people through computers, related equipment and other devices using media such as coaxial cable, telephone lines and microwave and satellite links for the purpose of information exchange and resource sharing. Information exchange may, for example, take the form of electronic mail (transmitting 'letters' over communications links) or participation in a public computer-based 'conference' (sharing viewpoints, etc. on a particular discussion topic through a data base comprising all the inputs from participants). Resource sharing may include the use of a distant computing facility, or access to a locally sited laser printer or the retrieval of information from a shared data base where the information itself is a resource.

Initially, computer networks were set up to promote the time sharing of large mainframe computers. Typically, the terminals were of the same type and there were as many physical connections to the mainframe as terminals on the network. The next step was to accommodate peripheral devices such as line printers and file stores, as well as extending the range of terminal devices and expanding the number of physical connections. With more terminal connections on the network than accesses (port connections) to the mainframe, users competed for ports and the use of the mainframe.

A logical extension of time-sharing systems is to communicate with more than one computer installation in order to share computing resources or stored information resident at a particular site. Figure 8.1

95

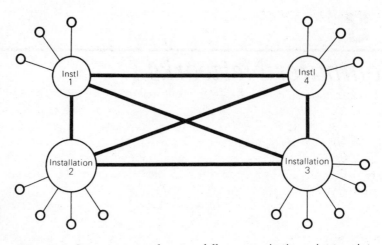

*Figure 8.1 Computer network system fully communicating point to point.
Small circles represent user terminals*

illustrates this concept. There are four computers (each supporting local users) that are interconnected to provide any user at any site with access to any one of the other three installations. From a terminal or microcomputer connected to the local mainframe a user can use raw computing power at another site, access a specific piece of equipment located at another installation (e.g. a computer output microfilm device) or retrieve information stored elsewhere. High speed data communications are necessary to facilitate the flow of the large volumes of data from one site to another which are not only fast but also reliable.

The merging of computer and communication technologies has significant influence on the way in which computer systems are organized. Networks are being set up, not only to share computing power, but also, and even primarily, to improve the flow of information within organizations and beyond.

Networking technology may be discussed in terms of three different methods of information transfer: *voice, data* and *video.* Organizations seeking to provide efficient and cost effective communication links may well wish to use all three. The technologies are essentially different but it is not uncommon for a network to combine two of the three (voice and data), and in some cases over parts of a network all three. Voice networking (the telephone) is the most common and accounts for most of today's networking traffic. However, our concern in this chapter is the rapidly expanding area of data communications.

DATA COMMUNICATIONS

The underlying method of operation for the transfer of data over networks is called **packet switching**. The data a user wishes to send, commonly referred to as a 'message', is broken down into smaller units called **packets** which are individually addressed and routed through the network. The packets are passed from one **packet switching exchange** (PSE) to another until they reach their destination. At each PSE, the packets are checked and retransmitted.

The difficulties in networking arise from trying to connect a whole variety of dissimilar equipment. For two pieces of equipment to communicate successfully they must 'talk' and 'understand' the same language. In the jargon, they must utilize the same **communications protocol**.[1] There are protocols for all aspects of the chain of communication from the cable and connectors used right through to the software running on the connected devices which controls the transmission of data over the network. We will not attempt to unravel the complexities of data communication derived from the use of diverse equipment nor dwell here on the application of protocols. These are areas of confusion even for experts.

Through the introduction of **local area networks** (LANs), organizations are able to interconnect their computers, terminals, work stations and other peripheral devices in an efficient and cost effective way using a shared communication link. Data communication is also possible on a broader scale (nationwide and worldwide) through **wide area networks** (WANs) which may interconnect different computer sites and branches of organizations in different towns and cities, and thus enable people miles apart to communicate with each other using computer equipment. Advances made in communications technology, notably in high speed digital communication and satellite systems, have made all this possible, but the success of networking on such an expansive scale depends on the creation, adoption and application of network standards.[2] Without these standards, there is no framework for development.

LOCAL AREA NETWORKS

A LAN normally serves a single premises or no more than a group of buildings. Just as domestic appliances can be plugged into sockets anywhere on a mains circuit at home, so computers and related equipment can be connected through nodes placed anywhere on a network. LANs vary considerably in extent (length or area covered) and

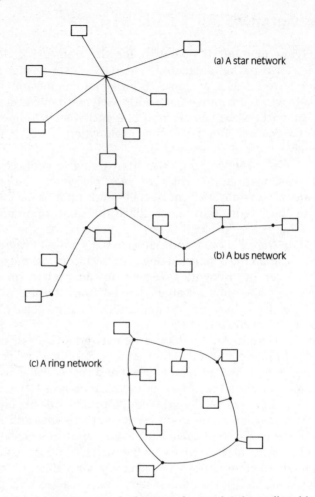

Figure 8.2 (a) A star network: this type of network is least affected by the failure of any of the connected devices or cables but it is clearly dependent on the health of the central point or 'hub'. At the centre of the star is a computer or a switching device. A star network is controlled centrally and in this way it differs fundamentally from the bus and ring networks; (b) bus network: this type of network fails completely if it is cut but not generally if one of the network codes is in trouble. When interconnecting a scatter of points on a site, a bus normally uses the least cable and adding another device to the network is quite straightforward; (c) ring network: this type of network fails completely if it is cut and it is vulnerable if there is a node problem since each node acts as a repeater. Redundancy can be built in by providing cable to by-pass each node

in the number of devices connected and supported. A local area network normally nestles within a spread of 1 km but may not extend beyond 20 or 30 metres. The number of devices supported maybe as few as 10 or as many as 1000. Rates of data transfer also vary considerably in the range 1–100 megabits per second (Mbs).

There are three basic shapes, or **network topologies,** employed in LAN design as illustrated in Figure 8.2. These are known as **star, bus** and **ring.** The differences in shape derive from the way in which each network operates. The selection of a particular topology depends on the sort of use for which the network is intended, the requirements of the organization concerned and the environment. There are advantages and disadvantages associated with each design. The more obvious factors influencing choice are the number of connections required, the physical area these cover and the distances between points, cable requirements and any specific installation problems, and future expansions.

There are three principal types of cable used in LANs: **twisted pair, coaxial** and **fibre optics.** Twisted pair copper cable (as used for telephone lines) supports only the lower bandwidth[3] but is cheap and easy to install. Coaxial cable generally carries higher bandwidths than twisted pair, is easy to connect into but is not so easy to lay (it doesn't bend readily). It is also more expensive. Optical fibre cable offers the highest bandwidths and is generally immune from electrical interference; however, it is difficult to install and comparatively expensive to purchase and lay.

There are two main categories of data transmission known as **baseband** and **broadband.** The baseband technique provides high speed transmission over short distances. It permits only one shipment of data at any one moment in time over a single data channel; however, the transfer of each block of data only occupies the channel for a minute period of time because of the high transfer speed, and by **multiplexing[4]** a number of transmissions it may appear that the network is handling traffic from different sources simultaneously. The LAN is essentially time shared using a mechanism of control which ensures that only one user is actually able to transmit data at any time.

The broadband technique is to transmit data using modulated carrier signals and thus a modem is needed to connect a digital device to a broadband LAN. The modem can handle a range of radio frequency carriers up to around 400MHz. This permits the use of several carrier frequencies, each providing a separate communications channel. A broadband LAN thus supports parallel transmission of data, and the method of transmission means that this type of LAN is able to handle closed circuit TV as well as data.

The Cambridge Ring

The **Cambridge Ring**[5] is probably the best known example of a ring network. Transmission of data is serial[6] and in one direction round the closed loop. Each device placed on the network is linked to the ring via a standard ring station or node. Any station can communicate with any other station by sending a **mini-packet** comprising a 'message' (i.e. the data to be transmitted) and the destination address.[7] Only a fixed number of mini-packets (themselves of fixed length) are allowed to circulate at any one time. A specific interface[8] is needed to link each different device using the network to a ring station. Significantly, a Cambridge Ring contains the flow control necessary to allow devices and software which operate at varying speeds to co-exist on the same network.

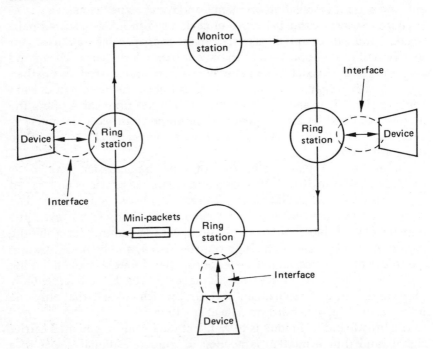

Figure 8.3 The ring system

The mini-packets are created by a monitor station and circulated round the ring passing through each ring station in turn. Each packet carries a 'marker' which indicates whether it is empty or full. Empty packets are free to be 'captured' (filled with data and addressed) as they pass through any ring station. A full packet then travels on round the loop until it reaches its destination as indicated by the address it is carrying. On arrival the data is copied to the target device and the full packet (now marked with a 'flag' to indicate successful delivery) continues round until it reaches the ring station where it was filled. The data it is carrying is then checked against the data originally sent. If there is a perfect match then the cycle is finally complete. As well as controlling the flow of packets the monitor station also logs the network traffic in relation to each device attached to the LAN.

The token ring

Another type of ring network is known as a **token-passing ring** or **token ring**[9] for short. A so-called 'token' is passed from station to station. When a station is in possession of the token the attached device is at liberty to transmit data. Each station manages its own affairs and hence there is no requirement for a separate monitoring station.

Ethernet

Ethernet[10] is probably the best known example of a bus-structured LAN. It consists of one or more segments[11] of coaxial cable to which are attached devices known as **transceivers**. Each device requiring connection to the network is joined through a transceiver which monitors network traffic and a controller which provides the interface between the equipment and the network. Data is transmitted in packets of up to 1500 bytes (destination and source addresses inclusive). The data transfer rate is of the order of 10 Mbs.

A connected device is able to send data if its controller finds that there is no other transmission in progress. The network is, of course, designed to guard against mishap should two or more devices believe the highway, or data channel, is free. Each transceiver contains a collision detect circuit which continuously monitors activity on the highway. If a collision is detected, the appropriate controllers are notified and the transmission ceases at that point. After random delays, the controllers involved look again to see if the channel is clear and retransmit the same data (starting at the beginning again). Destination controllers are also informed when any collision occurs and thus are alerted to ignore any corrupt packets which may arrive. In reality, because of the very high data transfer rate and well-controlled mode of operation, there is rarely a need to retransmit packets.

In practice, a business organization or company may require more than one LAN to service the proliferation and mix of computing equipment on site, and there may be good reason why the LANs are different in their topology. Word processors in one department, personal computers in another, terminals situated on the factory floor and mainframes in the data processing department may require separate networks. Most LANs installed today are small-scale systems to link microcomputers or electronic office equipment within a single department.

GATEWAYS

Although it may be desirable to set up separate local area networks for specific tasks there are also likely to be good reasons why some or all of the networks within an organization should be interconnected. Gateways are needed to perform this task. A **gateway** contends with any differences in packet sizes, protocols and addressing methods between the two networks it connects. Two similar LANs are connected by a type of gateway known as a **bridge.** Since, in this case, the two networks use the same protocols there is no requirement to modify the contents or format of the data packets as they pass from one network to the other. A bridge effectively combines two similar LANs to make one larger network whilst retaining the individuality of each network in terms of performance, reliability and security.

Gateways are also needed to connect LANs to wide area networks[12] which may utilize such services as those provided by British Telecom. In addition, WANs can be linked through gateways to create national and international data communication networks.

WIDE AREA NETWORKS

Wide area networks (WANs) are large-scale data networks which span a sizeable geographical area, normally based on conventional telecommunications techniques. Because transmission speeds and capacity are limited, data transfer rates on such WANs are appreciably slower than on most LANs. Wide area networks spanning considerable distances may use microwave transmission or even use communications satellites as routing stations. Such systems are extremely fast. A microwave network sends voice or data traffic by radio waves between relay towers.

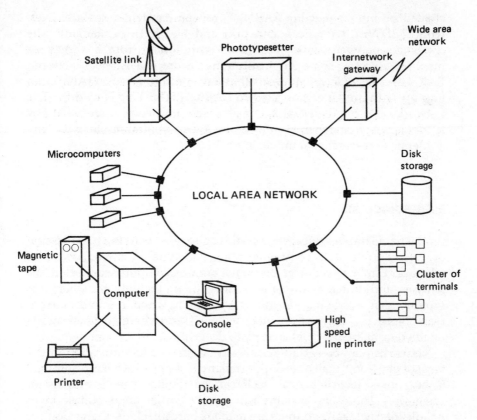

Figure 8.4 A conceptual drawing of a local area network indicating that a variety of computing equipment may be hooked into a LAN and that connection to a wide area network and satellite communications are possible

Each tower in the chain receives, amplifies and retransmits signals. Cable TV networks also provide potential for data communications.

World-wide data communications systems are of growing importance. They are vital to the working of the modern day financial world, linking for example the world's major money markets in New York, London, Zurich, Frankfurt, Hong Kong and Tokyo. Not all networks, however, are set up for purely commercial reasons. For example, academic and research institutions are amongst the principal users of WANs. Their currency is information in the pursuit of knowledge. Networks facilitate fast and reliable information exchange between institutions as well as supporting resource sharing.

Universities and polytechnics in the UK are linked through JANET (**J**oint **A**cademic **NET**work). A world-wide network for academic use is created by interconnecting EARN (European Academic Research Network), BITNET (American network) and NetNorth (Canadian). The combined networks link over 1200 computers[13] (from a variety of manufacturers) at some 350 institutions. There is a gateway between EARN and JANET which means that any site connected to JANET can link up with any site connected to EARN, BITNET or NetNorth. The networks also handle electronic mail which, in theory, means that any academic or researcher at university X can communicate with any academic or researcher at university Y.

ELECTRONIC MAIL

As the name implies, **electronic mail** is concerned with the transmission of 'letters' over data communications networks. A memo, letter or whatever can be keyed in at a terminal or microcomputer connected to a network and routed to any other connection on the network where it is typically displayed on a VDU for the person to whom it is addressed to read. Normally there is an intermediate store where the message is retained until the recipient is ready to deal with it.

Networks may be set up specifically to foster communication in the form of electronic mail or to support many tasks of which electronic mail is but one. Electronic mail itself can be divided into a number of categories. There are systems run purely within an organization to handle internal mail and there are mailbox bureaux like Telecom Gold. A subscriber rents a mailbox and is then able to send to and receive messages from any other subscriber. The system operates over conventional telephone lines and thus subscribers require a modem as well as a computer terminal. A mailbox is essentially a block of storage on the Telecom Gold computer system. A message which is addressed to you sits in your mailbox where it remains until you choose to check it out. There are also systems which, by way of interconnected networks (LANs and WANs), enable messages to be sent considerable distances, even world-wide, perhaps using satellite communication.

It is possible to get messages delivered immediately when using electronic mail which is obviously faster than the most efficient conventional internal mail service. There is, however, no compulsion on the recipient to read a message the moment it arrives. The person may not be in or prepared to deal with it at the time. The message is therefore saved and, normally, the next time the system is used it informs the person that there is a message waiting.

An electronic mail system is essentially a one-way system, e.g. it doesn't permit proper interaction as a telephone link does. However, it may provide faster access to busy people than the telephone. Just consider how often you telephone and find someone out or unavailable. Also consider how often you are interrupted by the telephone when you would really rather be left in peace to get on with whatever you are doing. Electronic mail allows both parties to decide when a message is processed.

There are a number of perhaps less obvious yet significant advantages derived from electronic mail. For example, it is easy to send multiple copies of a memo (essentially by associating it with a mailing list) and to forward a message to be read by someone else. Information from one message can be extracted and built into another document. All the memos, letters, etc., together with all the replies, can be retained on the system and filed electronically (as opposed to physically in paper form in bulky filing cabinets) for retrieval when required using some sort of keyword search (name, date of issue, subject matter, message number etc). Systems also typically allow a recipient to take a hard copy of any message which it would be useful to have in paper form by queuing (directing) it to a printer.

The first requirement of an electronic mail system itself is a guarantee that mail messages are correctly routed and that they reach their destination intact. The system is designed to inform a user that there is a message awaiting attention. It may issue a bleep at the receiver's terminal; it may flash a note on the screen announcing the arrival of a message (immediately or when the terminal is next idle); or it may let the recipient know next time he or she attempts to use the system. In addition, the sender of a message needs to be able to check that a message reached its destination and whether it has been read (accessed) or not. However, although an electronic mail system is designed to guarantee message *integrity*, it is unlikely to be totally secure. The very openness of a mail system makes absolute protection well-nigh unobtainable. Thus electronic mail may not be considered appropriate for handling confidential messages or sensitive information.

Facsimile (FAX) systems provide business with a special type of electronic mail delivery. The FAX equipment is capable of scanning a letter or document and transmitting it (inclusive of graphics and pictures) via telephone lines to another FAX station in another building, or in another organization, in another town or country where a copy of the original document is recreated for distribution or use at the receiving site. Facsimile transmission between continents may involve satellite communication. Typically one FAX station serves the needs of a whole business. FAX is a growth area. There are estimated to be over 1.5 million systems installed around the world (more than the number of telex machines which they are largely superseding). Some systems can transmit colour.

NOTES

1 A set of rules for hardware and software to facilitate communications and guarantee the integrity of data transmitted.

2 The international standard for the control of data communications between two or more computers or terminals using packet-switching technology is known as X.25.

3 Bandwidth is a measure of the information carrying capacity of a communications channel. The higher (wider) the bandwidth, the greater the capacity. Bandwidth is normally measured in Hertz (cycles per second), i.e., KHz (1000 Hz) or MHz (1,000,000 Hz).

4 Transmitting two or more data streams over a single physical channel. The two most common methods of multiplexing are frequency division multiplexing (FDM) and time division multiplexing (TDM).

5 Developed at Cambridge University but there have been several refinements made to the original design. The refined product is supported by a number of manufacturers but continues to bear the same name.

6 Serial data transmission is where the string of bits representing a character are transmitted following one after another along the same data channel.

7 A mini-packet is limited in the amount of data it can contain. In reality a series of mini-packets would be required to convey a proper message as we understand it.

8 An interface is needed to facilitate communication between devices which have different operational characteristics (e.g., speeds, codes, size of data blocks, etc.). The interface normally comprises hardware (e.g., a connection or switch) and associated software to handle the necessary conversion. A number of international standard interfaces and accompanying protocols have been established. One such interface which is widely used is known as RS232.

9 In this case the network does not have to be in the shape of a ring. You can have a tree shape or a bus shape which operates using the token ring technique.

10 Ethernet started life as a proprietary system, developed by Xerox, but the technology used is now widely supported by other manufacturers. The name is thus generally applied to LANs of similar design.

11 A segment is limited to 100 nodes and 500 metres in length. Thus a large network may consist of several segments joined together by repeaters. To build even larger networks, adjacent networks may be interconnected through gateways. A packet can only pass through a gateway if the destination is outside the network of origin.

12 A computer may perform the gateway role rather than a separate device. This is more likely in the case of linking wide area networks.

13 Discounting the multitude of microcomputers connected to LANs at each institution which may have access to the appropriate wide area network and hence the world-wide network.

9

Computer Applications

The computer is used to assist man in business organizations, in research and in many other walks of life. In this chapter we shall examine some of these areas in order to give an indication of the very wide range of activities in which the computer is involved. Some may be surprising, if you consider the limited capabilities of the machine. However, versatility has been provided by man's ability to reduce what are often highly complicated problems to the simple level at which the computer can be used, and to design and implement ingenious computer systems which can provide a myriad interplay of the basically simple tasks that the computer can handle.

You should remember that what has been achieved so far has been accomplished in a very short period of time. The first computer was developed as little as forty-three years ago and ten years passed before the industry was established on anything like a firm footing.

SCIENTIFIC RESEARCH

We have seen that the first computing projects were undertaken in university laboratories and scientific institutions to develop computers for special purposes. In science, the advent of computers has meant that calculations which were previously beyond contemplation, because of the time-span and drudgery involved in carrying them out, have now become possible. This has greatly accelerated and expanded research in such sciences as physics, chemistry, astronomy and genetics. More recently there has been an increasing use of computers for research and data analysis in less mathematical areas such as medicine, the social sciences and even the humanities where applications include concordances, textual criticism and stylistic analysis.

Computers are now a standard feature of life in universities and industrial laboratories, and, as we have seen, there are worldwide networks linking universities and scientific establishments (EARN and BITNET). Almost every branch of science and engineering has benefited from their development. Elementary particle physics is one field of study which has been broadened considerably. Molecular biology is another, resulting in spectacular progress in our understanding of the structure of living matter.

Because of the immensity of some of the research problems, huge computer complexes are sometimes needed. The CERN Institute in Geneva, researching in high energy nuclear physics, is one such centre. It is financed by a number of European governments, and has become an international pool of scientific brainpower.

BUSINESS APPLICATIONS

The first non-scientific use of computers concerned routine clerical work. Office administration had previously used such aids as punched-card accounting machines and adding machines. It was a natural progression to make use of computers. Computing procedures for clerical duties were relatively simple to develop since they were already well defined and the repetitive nature of many of the tasks made them very suitable for the computer.

Computer applications to business and commerce date from the middle of the 1950s, a decade of vigorous recovery from World War II which led to economic expansion and rapid technological development throughout the industrialized world. The pace of the technology has since quickened and today, most large and medium-sized companies are almost totally dependent on their computers for administrative functions. Smaller concerns are also heavily engaged in pursuing computing for themselves whereas previously they may have made use of the services of computer bureaux or had no involvement with computers at all. Micro-electronic technology is enabling offices to function more efficiently and the cheapness of the technology means computing is within the grasp of even very small businesses. Indeed, many a small concern probably owes its continued existence to improved efficiency and cost savings derived from the use of a microcomputer.

Payroll and personnel records

Payroll accounting was the first commercial area to become widely computerized. The calculation of wages or salaries involves a number of variable but common factors which relate to the personal details of each employee, such as gross pay or rate for the job, tax code, national insurance, etc.

These facts are retained on backing store together with information which accumulates each time the payroll is run, such as pay-to-date, and tax deducted for the year. Hours worked, overtime and any other information relating to the pay package being processed forms the input data for the particular run. The program contains formulae for calculating all the deductions to arrive at net pay. It will also build up records of tax-to-date, pay-to-date, etc. It computes these details, prepares a wages slip for the employee (and perhaps, a copy for the firm's pay office records) and writes up-dated information on the backing store for future use before moving on to consider the next employee. All this is integrated into one payroll system which may be made up of a number of related programs. They are not programs necessarily involving lengthy or complicated calculations but they save a considerable amount of repetitive manual effort.

If pay is made in cash, a program can include an analysis to calculate the exact number of notes and coins of each denomination required for the total pay out and for each individual wage packet. Another program might print out cheques to the individual bank account of each employee. **Files** generated by payroll are frequently enlarged to include such additional information as length of service, qualifications, training, attendance, sickness and vacation records, thus providing comprehensive personnel records.

The overall payroll system with attendant personnel details and records may comprise tens or even several hundreds of different though closely related programs and subprograms. Collectively they may form what is known as a package or even a set of packages. A software package may be a standard development (written in a common computer language) for use with a range of different computers and operating systems or it may be entirely home grown, written to the exact specifications of the business concerned. It may also essentially be a standard package incorporating specific local modifications to meet local needs. Increasing use, however, is being made of standard packages particularly where microcomputers are involved. Standard packages require virtually no on-site maintenance, i.e., they require no one to look after them.

Remember, computers essentially process information and it is only information, or rather data, which has to be provided to enable a package to operate successfully. A package is normally designed to accept data according to a specified format and the general aim is that the package should be easily usable by non-programming personnel. In the jargon, it should be 'user friendly'. With ease of use in mind, menu selection is frequently incorporated into the design of an applications package. The technique is to present the user with 'pages' of text which explain what to do at each stage of the running of the program. Typically the text, or *menu*, presents options which enable the user to select an appropriate course of action. In essence, the user does not need to remember what to do next. It is the responsibility of the software to prompt at every stage of the way. A 'page' of information is limited to the amount of text that can be displayed at one time on a VDU or video monitor.

The expense of a computer and the attendant system may not be justified for payroll and personnel records alone. The firm would probably use the computer for further analyses based on the payroll program, e.g., the relationship of total wage costs (weekly, monthly, etc.) to jobs in hand, total costs to date, individual job costing, etc. This kind of information, if quickly available and up-to-date, makes it easier for management to improve its efficiency by promptly pinpointing areas of weakness and strength. Up-to-date and accurate information can be obtained by consulting data bases.[1]

Office automation

Initially it was perceived that changes in office operation involving computers would be limited to clerical and routine functions of a repetitive nature. In the event, the technology and the science of computing advanced more rapidly than the business world at first thought possible and what started as a faster and more reliable way of processing payrolls grew to envelop the total business function. The convergence of computers and telecommunications, and rapid growth in the microcomputer sector, gave extra impetus to *office automation* from the early 1980s and contributed further to the gradual evolution of the *electronic office*.

Office automation can briefly be defined as the application of today's technology to today's office practice. In the application, various functions and practices inevitably change. The development of the humble typewriter[2] and the introduction of the adding machine[3] are examples of office automation from an earlier era. Today, office automation covers the use of stand-alone word processors, personal computers, work stations, terminals, various peripheral equipment, networks and FAX systems. It embraces document preparation, desktop publishing, electronic mail, document storage and retrieval, data and voice communication, business packages, information management, graphics and viewdata.[4]

Word processing

At a general office level, word-processing systems are commonplace. Word processors are particularly useful for preparing reports that may need to go through one or more revisions and for producing standard letters and documents. The software provides the capability to insert or delete words, lines or paragraphs, and to print out drafts and final copies at speed. No matter how many revisions are required the full text is only typed in once, i.e., the initial draft. Systems may include special purpose packages for specific applications such as merging address lists, producing a range of documents for quotations, purchase orders and invoices, and, very usefully, dictionary packages which signal and correct mis-spellings.[5]

A word-processing system basically consists of a typewriter-style keyboard, a processing unit with memory, a TV-type display unit (VDU), a magnetic storage device (typically a floppy or Winchester disk drive) and a quality printer terminal. The system also incorporates a package to facilitate editing, formatting and printing the text. It may be a single operator system or it may support a number of connected work stations. Increasingly, microcomputers are installed in offices to perform a variety of tasks. One of these may be word processing. In this case the word processing software or package is loaded into the microcomputer from disk storage when it is required. The word processing function is exactly as described for the stand-alone word processor above but there is the added advantage that the microcomputer can be used for other tasks, e.g., office accounting or information management using a database package. The special purpose stand-alone system is normally easier to use and often more versatile; however, the general purpose microcomputer with word processing software is becoming the more popular vehicle for word processing.

Desktop publishing

Desktop publishing is a major growth area in the field of office automation. This is not so surprising when you consider the vast quantities of material that business corporations publish every year (an amount which puts the major publishing houses in the shade) and then examine the considerable advantages which desk top publishing offers. By 'desktop publishing', we mean the process of producing any published material in an office environment from the creation of the text (words and graphics) through to page layout and design, and the production of the camera-ready copy complete with artwork.

As all the work is done in the office, the principal advantage is that anyone involved in producing published material is in complete control of the operation. Before the availability of the technology, the course of action was to mark up copy and submit it for typesetting in the hope that it would turn out as wanted. The whole process of publication is obviously very much faster as no external services are involved, apart from printing, when large print runs are required. Desktop publishing also considerably reduces publication costs.

A desktop publishing system is built around three components: a microcomputer, page makeup software and a laser printer. The microcomputer typically incorporates a number of other devices such as disk and tape storage, add-on memory and a graphics board. The page makeup software is what really makes it all work. It allows a user to set up, view and change page layout as many times as is necessary to achieve the right design. The software offers a range of fonts and character sizes, handles text justification, embeds graphics into the text and provides powerful editing features which permit changes to be made even at the page layout stage. The ability to zoom into any part of a page and to enlarge the selected area on the screen is typical of most systems. Whilst the software makes it all possible, it is the laser printer which makes it a practical proposition, for the laser produces low cost, quality output with a reasonable range of the same fonts you would expect to find on a typesetter. The quality may not quite be up to typeset standard[6] but it is acceptable enough for most of the work generated in an office environment.

Electronic office

There is much talk today of the electronic office. Office automation is fostering the evolution of the electronic office in which there is less emphasis on the written word (printed on paper) and more emphasis on retaining, manipulating and utilizing information in electronic form. As we saw in Chapter Eight, electronic mail can be an effective way of communicating without ever having recourse to paper. Also, electronic filing, indexing, archiving and retrieval of information can be practised effectively without the need for the retention of the information in a battery of filing cabinets. Information held electronically can also be presented in a form which aids decision making, for example, through the use of spreadsheets[7] and business graphics software.[8]

There are numerous benefits in pursuing office automation. These centre particularly around the productivity and quality of performance of clerical, secretarial and document preparation staff. Automation eliminates or limits such tasks as conventional typing, filing and indexing, miscellaneous form filling and photocopying. It should also bring about improved information dissemination and inter-personnel communication at all levels within an organization, and more effective planning and decision making based on the availability of up-to-date information and the ease with which it can be accessed and interrogated. In addition, there should be better responsiveness to enquiries and an improvement in the quality of customer documents and information.

For the benefits of office automation to bear full fruit, the various functions need to be fully integrated and, for this to occur, they must be in complete accord. For example, the accounts system may need to pass data to a corporate data base and the word processor may require information from the data base for assimilating into reports. The word processor should also be able to send prepared messages and documents to the electronic mail system for transmission.

There are also special purpose business systems tailored to meet business requirements and handle business applications. These utilize highly developed and highly tuned software packages which handle payroll and personnel records, office accounting, word processing, electronic mail, invoicing, record keeping, stock control, sales analysis and financial forecasting as appropriate to the needs of the business concerned. Specific hardware features may include specially designed terminals or work stations generally equipped with significant graphical capability.

Stock control and sales

Stock control, the processing of sales orders and sales accounting, sales analysis, market research, forecasting and subsequent production planning are all areas in which the computer assists in business and commercial organizations. In all these cases the company can benefit from the immediate availability of information which the computer provides.

For example, it may be a misuse of capital to hold more stock than is needed, but customers soon become dissatisfied if delays occur because of a shortage of stock. Automated inventory or stock control, as often practised in supermarkets, provides exact information at all times so that neither of these situations should occur through ignorance of the level of stock. It would be customary for each item in the inventory to be assigned a pre-determined minimum level. (This will take into account the rate of sale and the time needed for re-ordering.) When this figure is reached, the computer program outputs the information so that action can be taken.

When handling sales orders by computer, the present volume of sales is known and this information, together with past records and perhaps statistics obtained from market research, forms some of the data needed for sales forecasting, which in turn influences stock control. Basic information for billing (including discounts, shipping/postage costs, VAT, etc.) is obtained from sales orders and the computer can be used to maintain customer accounts and to print invoices. All these various applications make effective use of the machine's abilities to store large quantities of information and to retrieve items at speed, and they rely on program inventiveness to ensure that information is updated promptly, accurately and usefully.

The computer is also used more and more in everyday cash transactions. The intrusion on the public goes largely unnoticed. The cash register in supermarkets, stores and offices where goods and services are sold is no longer the traditional device it once was. Though looking similar, apart from more graceful lines, it is probably a computer terminal, sometimes referred to as a *point-of-sale* terminal, linked to a central computer, recording information about sales as well as providing exact change for the customer.

Banking

Banks were among the first large organizations to invest heavily in computing, and today banking is almost totally dependent on the computer. In the past, a large but manageable amount of bookkeeping was handled manually, but such has been the expansion in banking that a huge labour force would be needed to tackle today's massive volume of bookkeeping. The computer is necessary because there is no other way of dealing with the problem. In most instances, the computer is sited centrally. Branches are equipped with terminals, giving them an on-line accounting facility and enabling them to interrogate the central system for information on such things as current balances, deposits, overdrafts, interest charges, shares and trustee records. Under computer control, customer statements are prepared and printed out onto specially designed stationery. Cheques are handled by computers at the clearing banks, a mammoth operation normally carried out during the night when the system can concentrate on (be dedicated to) this purpose. The cheques are sorted into branch, and then customer order and returned to the branches the next day. The computer also provides each branch, and its customers, with prompt access to information from a much wider financial world than would be possible under a manual, local system. Developments, such as the automatic cash dispenser, are making it even easier for customers to deal with banks.

Leading international banks and financial institutions are able to obtain up-to-date news on foreign currency rates from the world's money markets using an on-line worldwide information retrieval service. London, New York, Zurich, Frankfurt, Hong Kong and Tokyo are the major sites in the network with each city servicing its own and neighbouring countries. Data is entered and received using visual display terminals, and the processed data is held on disk storage at the central sites.

Insurance and stockbroking

Insurance companies, finance houses and stockbroking firms also make use of computers. Here conditions and requirements are similar to those in banking. Large files of information have to be retained and updated, interest rates and bonuses have to be calculated, policy statements and renewal notices have to be prepared and payments made. In the buying and selling of stocks and shares, various calculations have to be made, contract notes drawn up and files consulted and amended.

The world of the Stock Exchange is changing rapidly. The traditional methods of trading involving brokers and jobbers are no longer practised. The Exchange is now a marketplace dependent on computers with share prices and records of share dealings maintained on data bases. Typically, dealers in stocks and shares work at desks with half a dozen or more screens and terminal devices. Some of them display up-to-date information about prices, transactions, rates of exchange, whilst others are used to provide administrative backup. Armed with this information the dealer is in a better position to apply judgement and take decisions.

In October 1986, the London Stock Exchange radically changed its mode of operation with the introduction of SEAQ (Stock Exchange Automated Quotations), a system which provides data about share prices for dealers and customers. SEAQ presents lists of all securities, together with buying and selling prices, and records details of all transactions. The actual buying and selling of shares is restricted to 62 companies, but the various information is made available in edited form to other Stock Exchange members and to investors through a viewdata service known as TOPIC. There are more than 7000 subscribers (TOPIC terminals) and the number is growing. Subscribers can look at information but not change it. Firms in the City may also be able to access SEAQ from their own computer systems.

An aid to management

We have seen that the computer is able to provide useful information. Let us consider what this means to people in managerial positions whose task is essentially to translate information into action. The immediate benefit is that the information provided is comprehensive and up-to-date. This means that decisions taken can be more reliable, and they can often be made in advance of a crisis, and thus perhaps prevent one, rather than after it has occurred. The computer can also be used as a management tool to assist in solving business problems. In **operational** (or **operations) research,** which is the name given to the application of scientific procedures to decision making, certain techniques are used which require the calculation and storage abilities which the computer can provide. **Critical path analysis** and **linear programming** are two methods of analysis which are used. These are applied in situations where a good deal of information is known concerning a number of variable factors, and where the task is to arrive at a solution which indicates the best possible relationship between the variables, taking into account whatever constraints there are. The **simulation method** is used where decisions have to be made on the basis of probability and where some of the information used in the analysis is itself predicted, and where past events have to be taken into consideration before arriving at a decision. In assisting in the decision-making process, the computer *uses* rather than *provides* information.

INDUSTRIAL APPLICATIONS

In industry, production may be planned, co-ordinated and controlled with the aid of a computer. The computer may also be used to direct the operation of individual machine tools (drills, lathes, saws, etc.) and also to operate assembly machines which piece together parts of equipment (e.g. electrical and mechanical appliances, sections of motor cars and even complete vehicles). The use of numerically controlled machine tools directed by computer-produced tapes can speed up production, ensure greater precision and reduce scrap wastage. In certain industries (chemical, oil refining) the computer can be used to monitor and regulate total processes (i.e., to perform process control) without human intervention, just as it can to control air conditioning and heating systems in modern multi-storey buildings.

The control of a chemical plant by computer is a much safer and more efficient method than by manual control, since changes in conditions which occur during a process can be detected and compensated for immediately. It would, however, be normal for human operators to maintain surveillance over the total process in order to intervene should the need arise.

Oil refining, the separation of crude oil into its many component oils is a continuous process and it depends on the maintenance of certain conditions throughout the process. These two factors make refining a suitable application for computer control. Instruments measure such variables as temperature, flow and pressure. Any deviation from the standard is detected and regulating devices are adjusted to bring the process back into line.

Electricity

Starting up a power station involves many complex operations which have to follow a strict sequence with set time limits between each operation. This is a laborious, time-consuming task under manual supervision but one for which the computer is well suited. The computer is also used by electricity authorities for load control. Demand for electricity is not constant throughout the day nor throughout the year. Generators have to be phased in and out to meet changing situations. Because of the time lag required to build up the necessary power, fluctuations in the load have to be anticipated in advance.

Under computer control, past records stored in the system, relating to changing hourly demands under various weather conditions, are scanned and compared with the actual, present loads in different parts of the supply network. Predictions are then made and generators are set to start and stop at certain times. This ensures that extra power is transferred to those areas where it is most needed at peak periods. It also ensures that those generators which have to be expensively fuelled with precious natural resources (oil, gas, coal) are not run wastefully when the demand for power drops.

Steel

Process control applied to certain parts of steel production has increased efficiency in the industry. One example is in the cutting of the steel into lengths to match the firm's order book. In the rolling mills, which run at great speed, red-hot steel billets are rolled out into strips. The billet size is not known accurately to begin with and, as each is rolled out, the length increases until the required thickness of sheet or diameter of rod is reached. Before the use of computers, the mill would cut the sheets or rods, of varying lengths, into standard sizes or a particular size for one order. The lengths of steel left over would be scrap which would have to be re-smelted, resulting in a lower grade steel. With the advent of computers, the amount of scrap was reduced to a minimum, for it became possible to calculate the lengths that the billets would make whilst still red hot and being rolled out. This information could be matched against a table of orders for the type and quality of steel being rolled, in time for the flying shears (computer controlled) to cut the strips in the best way.

Printing and paper

Computers are widely used by publishing houses and the printing trade where they are particularly useful in the production of newspapers, magazines and any other publications for which it is necessary to meet strict deadlines and where time is short. Journalists prepare their stories at work stations using a word processor. The completed articles are stored and eventually transferred for composition to produce the final layout of the newspaper. The typesetting is rapidly performed under computer control utilizing all the different type styles (founts) and character widths and depths (point sizes) that are necessary, dispensing with the traditional typesetting stage of the production process in which the type is set up manually.

Once text is in electronic form, it seems sensible to retain it in that form for future reference or updating. Journalists frequently require to search through archives to check previous articles and facts. An automated editorial library is able to provide a more efficient support service than the traditional library of clippings of individual news items manually marked up, cut out and filed. Reuters, the press agency that specializes in foreign news, now maintains an electronic library of its news stories. 'Reuters' Newsbank', as it is called, dates from July 1984 and it already contains over 550,000 stories. Staff in London and six other bureaux around the world, in New York, Hong Kong,

Johannesburg, Nairobi, Tel Aviv and Bahrain are able to access the data base and hence refer to any story quickly and easily. Pre-1984 stories, once retained as paper files, are now available for reference as microfilm records.

Publishers may archive complete manuscripts on magnetic tape or disk ready for reprinting or so that amendments can very easily be incorporated before reprinting. Computers are also used to update the listings in telephone directories, catalogues, and parts and price lists so that they can be quickly typeset whenever required.

In the manufacture of paper there are continuous processes, predetermined standards have to be maintained, and wastage has to be minimized. Computers assist the paper mills with process control in ways similar to those described in the chemical, oil refining and steel industries.

Engineering design

The design of any piece of engineering, whether an aeroplane, ship, car, bridge, road, building or machine should not merely be pleasing to look at. The piece of engineering must not only be able to perform the tasks intended for it over its economic or anticipated life, but it must also be able to withstand all foreseeable mishaps during its working life. Engineering designs, however sound they may seem to be on paper, have to be physically tested under simulated or real-life circumstances before becoming operational.

Computers can help in calculating that all parts of a proposed design are satisfactory as well as assisting directly in the design. If modifications are necessary and further calculations are required, the computer can evaluate the alternatives more quickly and more accurately than would otherwise be possible. This means a great saving in time and elimination of technical faults and human error (which could possibly be disastrous), before a design is further developed.

Computers are also used in calculations of space and layout as well as strength requirements. This not only helps ensure that engine parts are accessible for maintenance, and bridges and tunnels high and wide enough for unusual traffic; it also ensures that there is enough room for everything – passengers, fuel, cargo, etc. In motorway construction, the computer can calculate the amount of soil needed to raise an embankment, or the amount of rock to be removed in cutting through a hill, and it can work out the most efficient movement of such materials.

When fitting the structural and spatial requirements of an engineering project into an overall design, the computer can also help with graphical display, the creation of drawings and schematic diagrams. The facility to view a design from all angles while it is still on the drawing board, and then to be able to modify it quickly, avoids having to spend time and money building and testing several designs before determining which is the right one. The computer can provide graphical and perspective views to show the shape of a proposed aircraft wing or car body, the slope of a curve for a new road, the visibility that the pilot or motorist will have, or the accessibility of the instruments that he might have to operate.

Computers are also used as an aid to circuit board design, even assisting electronic engineers in designing circuits for other computers.

The application of computers to design is known as CAD (computer-aided design) and, where it applies specifically to engineering, it is often referred to as CAE (computer-aided engineering). CAD is dependent on highly developed and often very expensive software packages. There is also a heavy dependency on graphical hardware capability. In outline, the software provides the engineer with the ability to create, display and test a design, and to modify it as many times as is necessary. The display may be two or three-dimensional, a line or shaded drawing and in black and white or colour. A design can normally be viewed from different angles, enlarged, reduced and sections isolated and changed. At any stage, there may be a requirement to make a lasting copy of what is visibly displayed. This may be accomplished by plotting the display on paper or even copying it to microfilm. CAD/CAE software typically needs to be able to contend with all these tasks as well as handling all the calculations that are involved in proving a design.

CAD/CAE is normally practised on systems which are dedicated to the one purpose because of the extensive demands of the software. A system is typically based on a minicomputer or super micro and is set up as an individual work station. A quality, high resolution graphics display device is an essential component as is a hard copy output device which can match the sophistication of the display.

METEOROLOGY

Predicting the weather has long been considered something of a mystique based on country signs and folklore. Meteorology, as a science, is relatively young and, with computer assistance, it has become much more of an exact science. The problem with meteorology has always been to obtain sufficient data, and to analyse that data quickly enough so that predictions can be made. Weather is observed and data collected by human observers working at land stations and on weather ships, and by automatic weather stations on land and sea (moored or drifting buoys). Data is also recorded at different levels of the atmosphere using balloon-borne equipment and remote sensors carried on satellites. Readings and measurements are also taken from aircraft and commercial shipping. All this recorded data is transmitted to meteorological centres over telephone, radio and satellite links. Armed with more information, the relationship between the variable factors which constitute weather can be analysed in greater depth, and a more accurate prediction of future behaviour can then be made. The computer system is also able to analyse vast quantities of past measurements to test for weather patterns and, based partly on these results, long-range forecasts can be made.

The UK Met. Office has used computers for over thirty years. Besides handling forecasting for the UK, the Met. Office, through its massively powerful computer installation at Bracknell, provides an international service as one of only two world area forecasting centres.[9] Data collected worldwide is transmitted via a network known as the Global Telecommunications System, in which satellite relay stations play a significant role. Up to fifty thousand reports are received every 24 hours bringing details of such variables as wind direction and speed, temperature, atmospheric pressure and pressure change, cloud type and height, humidity, radiation, rainfall, visibility and weather. Besides providing public forecasting services (TV, radio and Weatherline), the Met. Office also provides forecasts for civil aviation and defence establishments. Other areas benefiting from forecasting and advisory services include the off-shore industry, agriculture, the building and construction industry and transport.

SPACE TECHNOLOGY

The development of space technology which culminated in the first moon landing was only possible because of the calculating powers and speed of the computer. Computers were used at the design stage of the project and in all phases of development right through to flight control. For example, they monitored and helped to control the proper functioning of all the equipment; they helped determine the routes (trajectory paths) and kept surveillance during the flight; they plotted courses of action when unforeseen events occurred; and, finally, they processed information relayed from the space vehicles.

The last point is significant because the collection of information is the main reason for putting satellites into orbit. Computer-linked space satellites provide previously unavailable information about the universe around us. This information is not merely of interest in scientific research (such as astronomy), but it increases our knowledge of our own planet (in geology and mineralogy), and it is of immediate practical value, for example, in meteorology. Satellites are also used as long-range beacons or microwave reflectors to provide the immediate worldwide coverage of important events by TV and radio that we now take for granted, but which were inconceivable even a generation ago. Satellites as we have seen are also used to provide worldwide digital communication links for data transmission. The computer has played a leading role in, and continues to be an integral part of, these wonders of the second half of the twentieth century.

COMMUNICATIONS

Air travel

Air traffic control, which is responsible for organizing the safe movement of our crowded airlines, depends on a significant amount of computer support. As flying speeds increase, control decisions have to be taken more quickly.

This also applies to the pilot who has to react not only to instructions relayed to him from traffic control, but also to changing situations during flight (variations in atmospheric pressure, wind speed and direction). Various instruments, dials and meters indicate the state of the flight and the current weather conditions. These provide the pilot and the flight engineer with the information they need to control the flight and to make navigational calculations. It takes time, however, to scan the instruments and to assimilate the information, and time can be critically precious at the speed at which the plane is flying. Small computers, made possible by the development of compact integrated circuits, are installed as part of the plane's equipment. These computers are programmed to continuously analyse data, which is relayed direct from the various instruments, and to provide co-ordinated information to the pilot in time for human decision and action. Control itself can also be invested in the computer so that, when certain conditions arise, automatic corrective action is immediately taken without the need for slower, human intervention.

Besides the many in-flight uses, the computer plays an increasingly vital role in the training of pilots. A flight simulator provides an exact replica of the flight deck and performance of an aircraft, enabling the equivalent of many hours of flying to be undertaken without leaving the ground. The computer resolves the tasks, monitors and controls the pilot's action, and maintains a record of the pilot's performance.

At ground level, the information needs of a busy airline are extensive. Computers are used for the efficient handling of seat reservations, crew schedules, timetables, tariffs, cargoes, maintenance schedules, personnel records, accounting, and stock control. Large scale air travel has developed quickly in recent years and computers have helped to make it a very reliable, and safe, form of transport.

Computer-controlled seat reservation brings benefit to customers and to the airlines. It is an economic necessity that airlines operate as near to capacity as possible. To avoid over-booking, a complete list of all bookings needs to be maintained and be available for immediate interrogation. This is achieved by using communication networks, covering whole continents, which link the booking offices to a large computer system working in real-time. Communication between continents is established by using transoceanic cables and satellites. A travel agent is able to find out the current status of any flight and can book seats on the basis of the information obtained. This is all done in a matter of seconds and, when a seat is reserved, the information system is automatically up-dated.

Computer controlled reservations are also applicable to travel agents, hotel rooms, theatre seats, and sporting events at large stadiums.

Transportation

Other transport facilities are making increasing use of computers. Railways prepare timetables, scheduling at the same time the distribution of the rolling stock to operate their services, and they control busy stretches of track with computer assistance. Shipping companies devise the best method of loading and storing cargo, using computer programs which are designed to take into account such variable factors as size, weight, solidity (the ability to stack in layers), destination and urgency. The computer in conjunction with radar and other monitoring equipment can also be used to make increasingly crowded shipping lanes, like the English Channel, safer. Haulage firms and transport concerns may determine optimum routing. If, for example, a vehicle has twenty delivery points, a computer program can consider all the various route options and pinpoint the shortest or the best route if other variable factors (such as avoiding travelling empty, combining several deliveries, refuelling) have to be taken into account.

Road traffic control

Maintaining the flow of road traffic in congested areas is of paramount importance and an increasing problem. The computer assists with the control of traffic lights in some of the world's major cities, and many more conurbations are likely to adopt this method of control. A single computer-based traffic system controls an area of some 200 sq. km. in Tokyo and the system is being expanded year by year. A similar system is in operation in London. Results are impressive if not always apparent to the motorist. Individual sets of traffic lights normally change after a set period of time, regardless of the volume of traffic. A network under computer control operates instead on the basis of the volume and flow pattern of the traffic at the time. Information regarding the volume, detected by measuring devices on approaches to all sets of lights as the traffic moves, is transmitted to the computer system. This information, representing a total overall view of the distribution of traffic, is related to permanently stored information regarding distances between lights and the permitted traffic speeds. As a result, the various lights over the whole network are changed to maintain maximum flow. Some systems can even trigger warning signs advising drivers of the optimum speed at which they can maintain continuous movement.

It is not unusual for television cameras to be installed at major traffic junctions so that potential trouble spots can be kept under surveillance. With pictures displayed from various vantage points, and a reporting system which indicates when a particular set of traffic lights has broken down, human operators can watch over the network and intervene when the occasion demands, promptly directing police and repair crews to the exact spot(s) where they are required.

LOCAL AUTHORITIES, CENTRAL GOVERNMENT AND PUBLIC UTILITIES

Local authorities, central government departments, and state-controlled public utilities all have to maintain extensive records. Indeed, in a socially conscious, heavily populated, industrialized environment, the tasks of officialdom today are of such a scale as to be impossible without computer assistance. The State is the biggest collector and collator of information in the UK, and the usefulness of the computer in storing, retrieving and analysing information is greatly increasing the scale on which it is collected. Computerization is also encouraging the centralization of information, for greater convenience and accessibility, in large data banks.

The computer is used extensively to carry out routine clerical functions, undertaking, for example, the preparation and printing of rate and tax demands, electricity bills and water rate demands. Computers are responsible for maintaining all driving licence records and for issuing renewal notices and licences. Similarly the registration of vehicles is handled by computers in regional centres. The computer is also playing an increasingly prominent part in the organization and running of the public health and social services, in the maintenance of law and order, and as an aid to eduction. Parliament itself uses computers in the preparation of *Hansard* and for the storage and retrieval of information in electronic form.

Telephones

Computerized telephone exchanges handle an ever-increasing volume of calls. They do so more quickly and with less likelihood of error than would otherwise be possible, and they can be linked up to other networks/exchanges for wider, prompt use. Cross-country, and even overseas, calls which previously meant a slow link-up through several switchboards and/or operators, can now be made directly and quickly. By way of satellites, calls can also be transmitted at faster speeds than through conventional networks. The computer can also maintain a log of calls for subsequent billing.

Medicine

The uses of the computer in the medical field are partly analogous to applications in business and industry. We find, for example, the computer being used increasingly in hospital administration for such tasks as maintaining inventories of drugs, surgical equipment, and linen; for payroll; hospital accounting; and for bed allocation. Information on the condition of patients, details of tests and clinical reports may be stored on a computer system. This combined information can be used to provide ward and patient summary reports and, where a terminal has been installed for the use of the ward nursing staff, the system can provide instructions and reminders concerning the care of individual patients.

In intensive care units, a computer can be used to monitor a patient's condition. Scanning instruments attached to the patient are linked on-line to the system so that nursing staff can be notified as the patient's condition changes. The computer may print out or display a log of the patient's condition, drawing attention to measurements that fall outside the critical limits set by the doctor, or the computer itself may trigger directly the necessary corrective action.

In some clinics, a computer is used, albeit in an experimental way, to 'interview' patients before or after they see a doctor in order to collect information for the patient's records and even to assist with the diagnostic process. It is suggested that patients are more relaxed, and honest and frank with their replies when faced with an impersonal machine.

The computer may assist in medical diagnosis, for example programs exist which can carry out electro-cardiogram analysis to determine both normal and abnormal heart conditions. The computer system can act as a vast encyclopaedia of medical knowledge, providing the doctor with access to an ever-increasing quantity of information which could not possibly be memorized. Diagnosis itself is a complex process, and the symptoms of a disease are not consistent in all patients. The consultant makes a human diagnosis on the basis of information gleaned from the patient's condition. In dialogue with the computer system, the consultant tests hypotheses (perhaps referencing other recorded cases) until completely satisfied that it is correct. The computer can help, but the experience of the consultant remains all important.

The computer may assist in prescribing the correct dosage and pattern of treatment, as, for example, in treating cancer by radiotherapy where it is vital that the correct dosage of radium is administered and only to the exact area required. Computers are being used to make these delicate calculations. Using data provided by the consultant, the computer produces a treatment timetable complete with the calculated dosage for the individual patient.

The computer has an important part to play in medical research and in teaching doctors and nursing staff. The ability that a computer system has to retain information on a large scale means that detailed records of case histories of particular illnesses can be available for scrutiny in sufficient quantities to assist medical research. Models can be constructed in the computer system to simulate the behaviour of various parts of the body, for example, the lungs and the heart. It is also possible to use computer programs to test the effect that a form of treatment might have on a patient before it is administered.

These different medical applications are in various stages of development. Some of the ideas we have discussed are not yet in widespread use, but enough has been achieved to indicate that the potential benefit of the computer, to both patients and to an understaffed and overworked medical profession, is considerable.

Law and order

The enforcement of law and order depends to an extent on the availability of up-to-date information. Police forces make extensive use of the information retrieval capability of computer systems for this purpose. Records are maintained concerning accidents, vehicle owners, disqualified drivers, traffic tickets, stolen vehicles, fingerprints, criminals, wanted and missing persons, stolen property and drugs. Some of these records are stored on microfiche. It is important for police in all regions to have access to these files of information and for response time to enquiries to be immediate; crime is not local and it does not stand still. A large network of terminals is needed with each terminal linked on-line to a large central computer system. Networks can be linked together, e.g. through Interpol, for fast, worldwide investigation of cases of international significance.

Computers are becoming commonplace in solicitors' and lawyers' offices for the purpose of legal data retrieval as well as for conventional accounting, record keeping, and preparation of legal documents. Typically, an office is provided with a microcomputer for local work and a terminal link to a vast data bank of legal information containing statutes, statutory instruments and accounts of past cases. A service organization is responsible for setting up and maintaining the data bank and lawyers who subscribe can conduct searches for information helpful to their clients' problems.

Libraries and museums

Increasing use is now being made of computers in library organization. Lists of borrowed books are maintained by the system and reminders for those which are overdue can be generated by computer output. A tally of the number of times books are taken out can be kept. More significant is the number of various ways that the contents of the library may be referenced with computer assistance for the benefit of users. Not only can all the books be classified by subject matter but, by page and paragraph references, information relating to particular topics within the subject can be pinpointed. This has particular implications for legal and technical libraries, where detailed references frequently have to be made and cross-references are of considerable value. Some university libraries in North America are linked to a network so that an obscure document in a distant archive can be quickly located and, in some cases, photocopies can then be faxed over a wide area.

Museums also make use of computers to help with cataloguing and indexing. Information about the exhibits in a museum's collection is assembled and retained as a large data base, and the information retrieval capability of the computer can then be exploited to the benefit of staff and visitors. Some museums are linked in a communications network to allow the exchange of information between different computerized museum data bases.

Education

The learning process can be enriched in many subjects because of the scale and range of information provided by computer data banks. Knowledge can be extended by the computer's ability to carry out lengthy and complex calculations at great speed. Use is increasingly being made of the computer as a resource in teaching and learning at all levels of education. Microcomputers are used by students in secondary education and increasingly pupils at primary level are being introduced to computers. Higher education, with its research activities, is supported by a proliferation of computing equipment and powerful installations. In addition, computers are used as a training aid in industry, business and commerce, and to help train people how to use computers and computer packages.

Instructional material can be prepared and stored within the computer in the form of programs which are carefully structured to teach specific lessons. Typically, some information is presented and then a question asked. Provided the correct answer is given the next step can be attempted. When the response is incorrect the information is repackaged and the question asked again. This drill and practice approach is known as CAI (computer-assisted instruction). This form of teaching aid has been used successfully to supplement more formal teaching methods and can be particularly useful for remedial purposes.

Software can also be written which encourages learning more by discovery and investigation than drill and practice. This approach is known as CAL (computer-assisted learning). Computer programs can be designed to create 'models' for experimental purposes (e.g. simulation of experiments in physics) which a student can use to discover what happens in given situations. The computer provides the opportunity for experiments to be carried out which would not otherwise be feasible because of dangers, costs, etc. Simulation programs can also be used time and time again with different sets of data so that a variety of conditions can be studied.

Students in higher education, particularly those studying science and technology, can also benefit from being able to use the computer as a computational tool. They may learn a programming language and write programs to solve some of their course work problems, treating the computer as an aid in much the same way as a slide rule or set of mathematical tables, or they may simply make use of a software package for which it is only necessary to provide data to obtain results.

The computer, can ease the load of administrative duties, leaving the teacher more time to concentrate on teaching. For example, the computer can be used to assist in building timetables; to monitor and schedule teaching resources; to build up and maintain comprehensive student records in order to provide a complete student profile; and to accumulate information for assistance with careers guidance.

Information systems

Computer-based information services for the general public are now available in the home, using the television screen as an output device. There are two broadcast **teletext** services, **Ceefax** (BBC) and **Oracle** (IBA), which provide several hundred 'pages' of up-to-date information as selected by the viewer by keying-in page numbers on a hand-sized control unit. The services are sent out on the same transmission as conventional TV programmes but a set with a special receiver, or an adaptor, is needed to pick up teletext. The services which are free cover such topics as weather details, travel information, financial news, the industrial news and the exchange rates as they fluctuate, the *Financial Times* index and the latest trends on the Stock Market, consumer news, and special events and happenings for the day, as well as important newsflashes as they are generated. At certain times of the day when the TV channels are not transmitting programs you can switch on your TV set and read Ceefax or Oracle pages which are displayed in sequence, changing after a set period of time. You do not need a special receiver for this but you have no control over what is displayed.

There is another and more versatile type of computer-based information system termed **viewdata** which is based on the telephone as well as the television.[10] The British Telecom version of the service is called **Prestel** and this service is based on a number of regional computers situated in various parts of the UK and one master system in London. Within two minutes of updating information on the master system it becomes available through the regional systems. The television is connected to the telephone by way of a jack plug and, as with teletext services, a key-pad is provided to enable the selection of information. The main difference between the teletext type of service and Prestel is that Prestel is a two-way system which allows the customer to carry on a dialogue with the computer system and the data base of information. For example, it permits a user to make a travel enquiry about a journey to a particular destination on a particular day, or to quiz a mail order catalogue to determine whether a particular item is available and even to place an order for the article. Unlike the free teletext services, there is normally a charge for accessing a page of information in addition to the standard telephone charge for the communication with the system. Information on Prestel is provided by independent agencies, including government and various business and industrial organizations, who lease space on the system from British Telecom. The information covers similar topics to the teletext services but, in general, does so more extensively.

A development of significance is **Mailbox,** an electronic mail service which enables subscribers to send messages to each other routed through the Telecom Gold computer system. There is a subscription charge which rents the mailbox (space on the system) and the message is sent for as little as the cost of a local telephone call. Other developments include the introduction of special viewdata keyboard terminals and business terminals which can have printing facilities attached to them, enabling the retention of information in printed form. It is possible to connect microcomputers and viewdata services to provide cheap and easy to use communication networks for businesses. It is also possible to connect local (that is private) viewdata and electronic mail systems, which operate within the businesses themselves, with the outside world.

*   *   *

Computers were evolved partly to meet the needs of war. They have been developed for peaceful purposes and have helped to bring the world closer together, to expand it, and to offer visions of other worlds which were previously unattainable.

The first computers were designed for a few specialized uses. Technological development has extended the range of uses, and today's computers encompass a wide spectrum of applications – warlike and peaceful, particular and general.

But knowledge brings responsibilities as well as benefits, and the social implications of the computer are discussed in Chapter Thirteen. Here, we have been concerned merely to point out the practical uses of the computer and to highlight some of its achievements. We should not forget that the computer, which is now an integral part of our everyday lives, has developed in less than a lifetime. Tomorrow? Who knows!

NOTES

1 A collection of information relating to a particular subject. A large data base is generally referred to as a data *bank*. The effectiveness of any data base of information depends to a great extent upon the efficiency and convenience of the means of access to the information store. The key lies in the structure of the data and the way it is interrelated. For efficient manipulation of data, increasing use is being made of data base packages and management systems. These may be large and costly pieces of software, meeting, for example, the requirements of an extensive technical library in a large corporation, or smaller packages designed to operate on personal computers, providing for the information management needs of a single office, with ease of use being a significant factor in the design.

2 The patent for a typewriter of a QWERTY keyboard was taken out by Scholes and Glidden in 1868. Remington started to market the device in the USA in 1873.

3 The Burroughs key-driven adding machine, complete with printing feature was introduced in 1891.

4 A system which enables the user to select any page of information from a central data base for display. In a business environment, for example, there may be a requirement to consult a financial data base for information about exchange rates, and so on.

5 More sophisticated software may check style and grammar as well as spelling.

6 The resolution of bottom of the range laser printer is 300 dots per inch (dpi) and that of a typesetter, typically 1200 dpi.

7 An application package typically designed to display and manipulate financial or statistical information. As the name suggests, the information is presented in rows and columns. A spreadsheet enables you to explore the implications of making changes to items of data and can thus be used as an aid to forecasting. Spreadsheets are associated with the use of microcomputers in a business environment.

8 Packages which display business information in a graphical form are becoming increasingly popular. Information depicted by graphs, bar and pie charts can be more readily appreciated and understood than presenting the same information as text or tabulated statistics. The software may operate with colour display and draw in 3D.

9 The other world centre is in Washington, USA.

10 Teletext and viewdata systems are sometimes referred to collectively as videotext systems.

10

Data Processing

Although computers were initially designed to solve scientific problems, the bulk of computing today is concerned with **data processing,** which covers a wide field of applications relating to commercial, governmental and industrial tasks, some of which were outlined in the previous chapter. Data processing 'probably accounts for between two-thirds and three-quarters of all computer people'.[1] The purpose of discussing data processing is not because so many computer personnel are engaged in this activity, but rather because it brings us back to a major concept, namely that computers process information.

So far in this book, the two terms *information* and *data* have been used interchangeably. There is, however, a difference between the two. The digits '070132' constitute data but they convey no information. They could be interpreted as a catalogue number, a date (7 January '32) or, as is the case, the dialling code from London to Hambledon – 070 132. The objective of data processing is to marshal or organize data into meaningful information. In this chapter we shall investigate what this entails.

DATA PROCESSING

Scientific data processing usually involves a great deal of computation (arithmetical and comparison operations) upon a relatively small amount of input data, resulting in a small volume of output. On the other hand, commercial data processing involves a large volume of input data, relatively few computational operations and a large volume of output. In the early days of computers, the emphasis was upon scientific data processing, but once it was appreciated that the computer

133

was not only a computational tool but also had the ability to store vast amounts of data, then commercial organizations became interested. In the United Kingdom, the J. Lyons Company designed a computer for their own business purposes (LEO) which became operational in 1951. In the United States, also in 1951, the UNIVAC machine, intended for both scientific and commercial applications, was the first machine to be widely used for data processing.

The processing of information existed long before computers. Every organization whether commercial, industrial or governmental, has always had a certain amount of paperwork. Before computers, this paperwork would have been processed manually and/or with the help of business machines. Within a computerized data processing system, however, information has to be structured so that, as data, it can be handled by a computer.

We shall now briefly examine the steps by which information (current and past paperwork) is expressed as data, processed, and returned to managers or other individuals, as updated and useful information. There are, basically, five steps:

- preparation of source documents;
- input of data;
- manipulation of data;
- output of information;
- storage of data.

Source documents   The first step is to obtain the relevant facts and figures and to set these out on source documents. For example, in a population survey, the name, address, age, sex, occupation, etc., must be first written down onto a survey sheet or some other document. These documents may be so designed that information is recorded in the same structure as the data required by the computer program.

Data input   Once the data has been extracted from the source document, it must then be transposed into some form suitable for entry into the computer so that processing can take place. The method will depend upon the input media or device, e.g. punched cards or paper tape, VDU, OCR documents.

Data manipulation   Information, input as data, for processing, may have to be *classified* or *sorted*. It is this form of operation, or data manipulation, rather than pure computation, with which data processing is mainly concerned. For example, in the population survey, we may want to classify people by occupation or by age. We may wish to sort lists of names or items in alphabetical order; or, in a social service environment, to list people to be visited by street order. We may require employees to be grouped by departments for a payroll program; or, in a job-costing program, to group the costs of all the elements that went into the manufacture of an item. This will involve some form of *calculation*, another example of which is the calculation of a weekly wage based on the hours worked times the rate of pay. All these forms of data manipulation will produce results, results which can be organized in the form of *summaries*, e.g. the numbers of adults and children in a given district or street, or the numbers of children of school age and of those under school age.

Output of information   The objective of outputting results or summaries is to provide meaningful information to managers, accountants, population survey analysts, and so forth. Careful consideration, therefore, should be given to the *presentation* of results so that they can be digested easily and quickly. With the first flush of data processing by computers, everything which could be generated was often printed out, resulting in pages of figures which, by their sheer volume, became confusing. Even summaries can be hard to read if they are not clearly laid out. People receiving computer output have been forced to think out more exactly what information they require from the computer and how it can be presented most usefully.

Data storage   In most cases, the results of processing one set of data are retained for future use or reference. For example, in a payroll program, last week's updated results will be needed by this week's program in order to update the 'gross-pay-to-date' total. In the other examples cited, it may be necessary, after updating, to compare the latest figures with previous figures, perhaps over different periods of time (sales analysis). This means that data processing installations require a great deal of secondary storage space to store all the programs and the different sets of data.

FILES AND RECORDS

Data relating to a specific application, for example, payroll (or inventory control, sales analysis or invoicing to customers) is organized as a separate **file**. Each file is made up of a number of **records** which, in turn, contain a number of **fields** or **properties**. On a payroll file, comprising the many records of everybody on the staff, each record will have certain fields to represent the individual employee's name and number, department, gross pay, National Insurance contribution, income tax code, etc.

Each record in a given file has the same structure, i.e. the same number of fields, with a given field in each record always containing information about a particular property, e.g. the fourth field always contains 'Gross Pay' and the sixth field 'Income Tax Code'.

There must be some method of being able to select one particular record from all the others. This is possible by choosing one of the fields as a *key*. For example, if the police are interested in the details of a given criminal on their criminal records file, the obvious **key-field** to look under is the criminal-name-field, since this will be unique for each record. Similarly, in a payroll file, the key-field would be the employee-number-field or, in a banking environment, the unique customer's-account-number-field.

Once the initial information (from the source document) has been entered via some input device as a file of individual records, this is usually copied onto magnetic tape or disk, so that when the information is required by a program, it can be transferred more speedily into main memory. In the case of direct input via a teletypewriter terminal, the records would go straight onto disk.

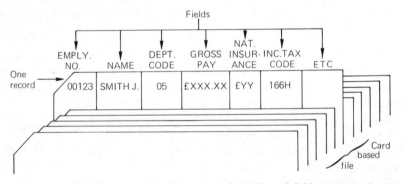

Figure 10.1 A record, of fixed length and number of fields may require several cards to contain all the necessary information. The concept of files and records was related to the original standard punched card

It is customary to set up a **master file** of permanent (and, usually, the latest) data, and to use **transaction files** containing data of a temporary nature. For example, the master payroll file will contain not only all the permanent details about each employee, his name and number, income tax code and so forth, but it will also include the current gross-pay-to-date total and the tax paid-to-date total. The transaction payroll file will contain details of hours worked *this* week, normal and overtime, and, if piecework is involved, the quantity of goods made. When the payroll program is processed, both files will have to be 'consulted' to generate this week's payslips, and the master file updated in readiness for the following week.

A file may have to be searched or consulted in more than one way. This can be illustrated by reference to a police file containing records of criminals. Each record will have fields indicating physical characteristics (height, weight, sex, age, colour of hair, scars). It may also have fields to indicate crimes committed (type, when, where and how) and other details concerning the criminal's background, haunts and acquaintances. If the police are interested in a particular person, they can access the master file by the person's name (a unique field), but if they are looking for a type of suspect (e.g. a female, 6 ft tall, red hair, over forty), they can access the file by the characteristics of a physical description, using several fields. A search program can scan the records on file and produce a list of all those who fit the required description.

The weakness of some data processing systems is that whilst they work for most of the time and for most situations, the exceptions are overlooked. An effective system should anticipate all likely and foreseeable contingencies. It is necessary to consider in advance very carefully everything that may be required – the amount and type of data and how it may be manipulated – so that the structure of each record will be adequate for *all* circumstances. Files will be updated and amended, but to alter their structure at a later date is usually very troublesome.

The various processes carried out on files may be summarized as follows:

File creation This is the method of organizing one's data for use by the computer system into a series of records of a particular length, content and layout.

File access When the particular application program is in use, it will have to access the relevant file(s). Since each file may contain a great deal of data, it may not be possible for the entire file to reside in main memory and portions of it will have to be drawn from secondary storage as required. A part of the operating system known as the file management system takes care of this activity. It is able to pass a certain number of records into main memory, to know when these have been processed, to transfer them back to the storage device, and to usher in some more.

File manipulation and maintenance Having accessed the file, the individual records will be processed in some way (sorted or classified) but, in addition, other records may have to be added or deleted (a payroll file will need to add and delete employee records as people join or leave the company). In some cases, all the records on file may be printed out; in others, perhaps only selected records would need to be printed.

File generation   As a result of the manipulation of data in files, new files will be generated. Once an existing file has been altered, it is necessary to create a new file by writing the updated (altered) file on a new tape or another area of disk. The old tape or area of disk can then become available for re-use.

File organization

The address of a record, that is, its place within the data processing system as a whole, depends upon the type of storage used. In Chapter Four we discussed sequential and direct access. Let us consider these terms again as they relate to file organization.

Sequential   Records on magnetic tape are arranged in a sequential order. The only way to get to a particular record, say the third one, is by passing over the first and second. In other words, the program has to start at the beginning of the file and work through it. This means that the program must 'look at', in some sense, each preceding record to see whether it is the one required. This is costly in time when only one, or a few, records need to be accessed and illustrates one disadvantage of magnetic tape. Another is the fact that three or four tapes are required to perform a sorting procedure.

Direct   With the development of magnetic disks, some of the disadvantages of sequential file organization were overcome. Direct file organization enables the program to have immediate access to the record required. The program need only inform the file management system which record is needed and from which file, and the management system then searches through the filing system and produces the record. Because magnetic disks allow direct access, as well as having a faster rate of data transfer, records can be accessed more quickly than is possible for magnetic tape.

Direct file organization is usually the better method when the need is for immediate processing of small quantities of different records at irregular but fairly frequent intervals, i.e., in airline reservations, banking, etc. When entire files, or the majority of records have to be processed (e.g., weekly/monthly payrolls, quarterly stocktakings), it is usually cheaper, and sometimes as fast, to use sequential file organization.

There is another method of getting to or storing information in a file, called **indexed sequential access**. This is the process of storing or retrieving information directly, but only after reading an index to locate the address of the item of information.

Efficient data processing depends on a clear analysis of what the user requires. How such an analysis is achieved and how the user's objectives can be met is the subject of the next chapter.

NOTE

1 An industrial view as quoted in *Computing Science Review*, Science Research Council, June 1972, p.53, section 9.2.

11

An Introduction to
Systems Analysis

A national newspaper once reported 'Computer Makes Firm Bankrupt'. Such a statement is misleading since it portrays the computer as some malevolent beast wishing harm to its owner. But the fact remains that the company did become bankrupt after installing a computer. We can also quote a computer system in the USA which recorded details about every suspect (innocent or guilty) picked up by the police. If a person was 'booked' again, at a later date, details of any previous criminal record would be readily available. This system, however, failed to delete information when a suspect was *not* convicted. Thus any policeman checking through the file could be given useless, and possibly prejudicial, information about innocent people. Why do these situations arise and how can they be avoided? We cannot blame the computer, nor can we always blame the programmer.

There is one large area within the computing process which we have not yet discussed. People tend to think of there being a problem (payroll, control of traffic) which is tossed to a programmer with a curt 'Now go away and make the computer do it'. The procedure is not as simple as this. Just as we saw that the computer is surrounded by an intricate web of software, so the procedure for computerizing a problem is made more complex by a large area which we shall call 'para-computing' (see figure 11.1), and of which **systems analysis** forms the major part. One of its main functions is to convert an existing manual system into a computerized system, or, indeed, to improve and extend an existing computerized system. What the systems analyst has to produce, then, is a highly detailed design which defines exactly how the new system is to work. If this design is flawed, then the type of situations described above can easily occur.

THE DEVELOPMENT OF SYSTEMS ANALYSIS

Systems analysis goes back to the late 1950s, at which time commercial organizations began to make use of computers with especial success in one area, namely, company payrolls. We know that a computer requires accurate and detailed information before it can carry out a task successfully. Since the payroll procedure, as a manual system, was so clearly defined, it was a relatively simple matter for a programmer to convert the payroll procedure into a program. However, difficulties emerged when the same programmers were asked to computerize other parts of a business system which were less clearly defined, for example, stock control, sales forecasting. They could perform the programming, but not the process of converting a manual system into a form in which it could be programmed.

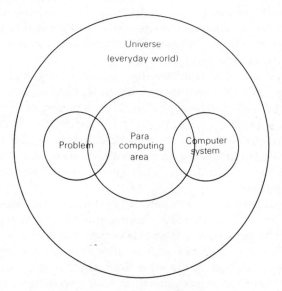

Figure 11.1 In addition to systems analysis, para-computing also includes data collection and data preparation

What was needed was a specialist, someone who understood both the computing and the business side of the total process.

The whole subject of systems analysis has undergone many changes since the early 50s. Today, the terms *consultant, analyst* or *systems developer* are used in preference to *systems analyst* which in practice described just part of the work. An existing system has not only to be analysed but also designed and, later, implemented and tested. In turn, as the applications themselves became more complex and demanding, individuals tended to specialize in one or other of the separate stages. This led to a growth of consultancy firms which could call upon a team of highly experienced personnel to carry out some overall task.

It is not just the job titles that have changed over the years, but the entire methodology. As more complex tasks were put forward for computerization, so the tools at the analysts' disposal had to be improved. The old *ad hoc* methods, based on experience gained from previous jobs, were not capable of defining the overall design clearly enough. Today, much more structured techniques are employed and require a specialist study. Here, we mention some of the more common approaches.

Structured systems analysis and design methodology (SSADM) employs diagrams in the form of dataflow diagrams, data dictionaries, etc. which are easier to understand than the written word. Accurate communication between the analyst and the user of the system is essential. Both the analyst and the user, not to mention the programmer, can more easily appreciate the design details when these are in the form of structured diagrams.

The analyst may communicate their systems designs to the programming department via a variety of techniques. Most are based on varying levels of charts. The top level gives an overall picture of the total system, the lower levels bringing out more and more detail. Structured charts, HIPO (hierarchical-input-process-output) diagrams, Michael Jackson Structured charts, psuedo-English charts, Warnier-Orr diagrams, etc., are some of the more common techniques used and forms the so-called *top-down approach.*

It is not possible to examine and discuss the details of these techniques in this text; the reader is encouraged to browse around some of the larger bookshops to see what is currently on the market. What we attempt below is an outline of the various stages in the development of many applications and, at the same time, show how the analyst acts as an interface between the organization which requires computerization of some company practice, and the DP department which will eventually be responsible for its implementation and maintenance.

This approach implies some large organization which may well spend hundreds of thousands of pounds each year on its computer department. To spend part of this budget on highly skilled and expensive analysts, whether from within the organization itself or from outside consultancies, does not seem to be out of proportion compared to the total annual budget. However, when a far smaller organization spending perhaps as little as £500 on the hardware has to pay perhaps ten times this amount for the analysts' services the cost-benefit is more difficult to justify. Hence, smaller companies and businesses tend to take short cuts to avoid spending such sums on analysts' fees. This frequently leads to disaster and, eventually, a much more costly expenditure when the application fails to meet with the original intention.

The moral is that, when computerizing an existing manual system or, indeed, altering an existing computerized system, it is better to pay the expert's fee and be reasonably content with the result than to skimp on this vital stage.

In general, hardware is cheap and forms a minor part of a complete computer system. It is the software that is far more important since it is this which produces the results. The better the software, the better the results.

The analyst's relationship to the company

One of the primary activities of the analyst within the company is to communicate with top management. The decisions about what will be computerized, and to what extent, will have to be taken by management in the light of the report, or *feasibility study*, presented to them by the systems analyst. At this stage, the analyst is only concerned with helping management to make the correct decisions.

The analyst will have to work with every department in the company which might be affected by computerization. No new system can hope to be successful until its effect on other departments has been carefully measured. To do this, the analyst has to *gather information* from the company's personnel and here, of course, the problem of human relations is raised. Some workers may think that the systems analyst is trying to replace them with a computer! It is not unknown for false information to be deliberately given because of this fear. At the very least, the work done by the analyst results in changes of working practices and conditions which could lead to problems with individuals, trade unions and so on. Tact, a maturity of understanding, and an ability to *communicate* with people are essential to the analyst.

He has to meet both management and company personnel to present a clear explanation of their new role arising out of computerization. This includes educating or retraining people in their 'new' practices.

The analyst's relationship to the computer department

Although the systems analyst is often found working within the

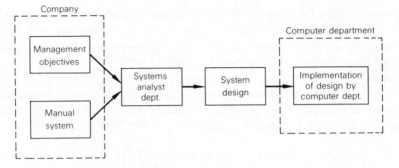

Figure 11.2 Inter-relationship of the analyst's work between the company and the computer department

computer department, conceptually his duties place him in a position midway between the company and the data processing department. He has to rely on the computer manager, the programmers and other DP (data processing) staff to carry out the systems design. Good relations with the department are therefore important, and friction could occur if it is not clear who is responsible for which aspects, even down to apparently trivial details, such as:

- the choice of programming language;
- keeping within the schedule and budget;
- who may contact client departments directly about details in records.

Communication between the analysts and the rest of the company, particularly the programmers, requires *formal documentation*. This simply means a highly detailed record of what the systems design must achieve and how this is to be carried out using current structured systems analysis and design techniques. The precision of detail required is fully appreciated often only by those actually involved. For example, if a certain field in a record is used to enter an employee's gross weekly wage, then the program will interpret whatever is found in that field as the gross wage, even if the person's date of birth is placed there in error. Formal documentation serves not only to show the programmer for what purpose certain fields are to be used, but also the other departments who have to fill them in, and it also indicates how they are to do so. Any flaw in this documentation can have disastrous results. One small example may illustrate this point.

An American mail order firm sent magazines not only to their home market but also abroad. One English recipient was surprised to find his magazines had suddenly stopped coming. He subsequently learned that the company had decided to computerize their mailing system and that, in the change over, no room had been left on the computer address records for the country of destination. Consequently, no magazines were posted overseas!

To the layman, such an obvious oversight is incredible: yet this sort of thing can happen so easily. There are many such anecdotes, and not only from the early days of computerization. This story may help us to understand the depth of detail into which the analyst must go.

Background knowledge required by analysts

A wide background knowledge of both business methods and computing is essential to the systems analyst. No one person can be expected to be skilled in all fields and there is a tendency today, especially in large companies, to re-define systems analysis into two roles. The *business* analyst who specifies the system design (in non-technical terms) and the *technical* analyst who takes the specification and assumes responsibility for the design problems associated with the computer system.

The business analyst would have to be familiar with some of the following subjects: business structure, organization, management and administration; production planning and control; stores and stock control; accounting; operational (operations) research; conducting and analysing surveys; simulation and model building. Whereas the technical analyst should possess a knowledge of the techniques of data processing, programming, computer operations, computer systems (including the current cost and performance of both hardware and software); and he should be able to advise on the relative merits of I/O and secondary storage most appropriate to the company's needs.

INITIATING A SYSTEM

Suppose you are in a non-computerized organization, or that you have a problem which could benefit from the use of a computer. Where do you begin to find out whether you really need a computer, which system, or what hardware and software to use? You would approach a systems analyst, either through your own DP department or through one of the consultancy agencies.

Let us now draw up a possible, and admittedly ideal, framework showing the sequence of events which takes place when a computer system is proposed. The steps involved are:

- assignment brief;
- steering committee;
- feasibility study;
- full system investigation;
- design, implementation and testing.

Assignment brief

Top management briefs the systems analyst as to the objectives of the proposed system. It provides the necessary authorization for him to investigate files, to enter other departments and question personnel, and assigns company staff to help the analyst in his investigation.

Steering committee

The analyst must meet and discuss the overall objectives given by top management with other members of staff. This is done in committee with the managers of all the departments involved, the analyst and, if one has been appointed, the DP manager.

Feasibility study

As the name implies, it is a survey of the possibility of computerization based on management's objectives related to an analysis of the existing facilities within the company. The resultant analyst's proposal may be to go ahead with computerization; *not* to go ahead (i.e. the existing system would not benefit by computerization – honesty is required here by analysts, especially if brought in from an outside organization); or, to defer the matter because it is impractical at the present time. Feasibility studies tie down company personnel so they are concluded as speedily as possible and, whatever the decision, the analysts have to be paid. If the survey concludes that a computerized system is not necessary, or that the original objectives are not attainable, the reasons are clearly stated, but if it appears that a computer system is feasible, the study will bring out the following points:

(a) What are the likely problem areas which will need special attention?
(b) What are the likely computer configurations which would be suitable?
(c) What are these configurations likely to cost in terms of money, staff and time – to design, to install, to test, and to run?

Full system investigation

If management concludes that it should go ahead with a particular system, or further explore several alternatives, the systems analyst will then prepare a detailed design, or several proposals, which must be complete in every probable and possible detail. Failure to do so will court disaster. It should be emphasized that once a particular system has been selected, one tends to become tied to it. It is often impractical to change a system drastically at a later stage. The analyst should ensure that what appears to be practical now will be capable of providing, or incorporating, the possible modifications that may be required subsequently.

Design, implementation and testing

Most computer systems are implemented on a modular basis, i.e. the overall design system will be broken down into a series of sub-units (modules), each one being thoroughly tested before becoming operational. As each module proves to be satisfactory it will be integrated into the developing overall system. Ideally, both the manual and the computerized systems should run together side by side until everyone concerned is satisfied that 'all the bugs have been ironed out'. This is expensive and does not always happen. When it does, the kind of nightmares described earlier are invariably avoided.

The most important point to be appreciated from this chapter is that for successful computerization, the process cannot be left entirely to the computing professionals. A dialogue must exist between the computer specialists and those directly involved. With the right kind of dialogue, computerization cannot but help all concerned. A respected doctor/ lawyer is one who, amongst other things, takes the trouble to *explain* an illness/problem to his patient/client. Strikes are better resolved when both sides really understand each other's problems (and fears). When it is a question of computerizing some system which affects the whole of society (e.g. the collation of all known facts about an individual in one central file – the privacy issue, and see Chapter Thirteen), then it is essential for everybody concerned to be involved in the discussion.

12
The DP Department and Information Centres

A company or business organization may require the services of a data processing (DP) department, depending on the size of the organization and the extent to which computers are used. The personnel involved may be as many as a thousand or as few as half-a-dozen. The structure of a DP department depends on the nature of the business computerized and the number of staff employed. Some organizations may handle all their computing requirements in-house whilst others may use the services of a bureau for some activities, for example to write software to meet the special needs of the organization or even to provide raw computing power.

Originally, many businesses opted for bureau services because they had insufficient work to justify the cost of setting up their own computer installations. Today many of these businesses now fend for themselves totally, or at least in part. This is because of the significant reduction in the cost of computer hardware and the availability of a much wider range of quality software packages, including special business systems. However, whether the data processing is handled internally by the company, through a single department or otherwise, or externally by a bureau, there are three major areas of involvement for personnel. These can loosely be described as design, development and operation. However, small organizations may purchase total packaged systems and only be involved with operation.

DESIGN (SYSTEMS ANALYSIS)

In the previous chapter we discussed the role of the systems analyst. In a large organization there may be a group of such analysts, headed by a *senior systems analyst* who would be primarily concerned with establishing the need for a computer based system and, subsequently, for directing its design. The analyst, or team of analysts, (who may function outside the DP department), would prepare detailed specifications of the problem in a form suitable for the programming staff to interpret. The senior analyst would draw up plans in clear and concise terms, maybe in block diagram form, outlining the main sections of the computer solution. Other members of the group would then expand these in much more detail.

Before a system can become operational, the systems analyst arranges trial runs with suitable test data. It may be necessary to organize courses and to prepare instruction manuals that explain to personnel the procedures for the collection and preparation of data. Once a project is implemented, continual assessment is necessary to ensure that the system continues to meet its original specifications.

DEVELOPMENT AND MAINTENANCE (PROGRAMMING)

Most organizations that require computer services will need a suite or range of programs, e.g. covering payroll, stock control, production control, customer accounts, and whatever other operations are appropriate. These may be provided as packages by the manufacturer or written by a software house or bureau to the exact specifications provided by the organization (the systems analysts plans), or developed in-house. On a large project, a group of programmers works together as a team with each member responsible for one part or sub-section of the end product. For this to work efficiently, standards have to be agreed and conscientiously followed by all members of the group, and timescales have to be met.

A large team is led by a *programming manager* who specifies individual responsibilities as well as timescales for each stage of development. In addition, the programming manager is responsible for the efficiency of the operating system software. Normally, support for the operating system is provided by the computer manufacturer, or by a company to whom the manufacturer has delegated responsibility.

There are two broad categories of programmer; production or applications programmers, and systems programmers. A programmer may practise at both levels, particularly in smaller organizations.

The *applications programmer* normally works from outline designs provided by the analyst and follows operational plans drawn up by the programming manager. The applications programmer is concerned with the construction of a step-by-step solution and the subsequent coding and program testing, and is likely to work in a high-level language, e.g. COBOL for a commercial application. Responsibility may also extend to the installation and maintenance of packages purchased by the organization, and to the support of their use in-house. Some applications programmers specialize, in graphics for example, and there is a new breed of specialist associated with data bases *(data base controllers)*.

It may be that an installation can rely almost entirely on the system software supplied by the manufacturer but, in all probability, it will be necessary to add system utilities to suit the special requirements of the local environment. The maintenance of the operating system, and any changes and additions that are deemed necessary, is the responsibility of the *systems programmer*. In contrast to the applications programmer, the systems programmer must have a working knowledge of the language of the machine (assembly code) which will be used.

Considerable emphasis is now placed on the development of standard software packages to meet the standard requirements of a range of customers. Such software is developed by the software divisions of the computer manufacturers and by software houses and bureaux rather than by programming groups working within specific data processing departments. An increasing number of analysts and programmers are employed in this sort of activity and the market for applications software is still expanding.

OPERATIONS

The day-to-day running of a computer system is centred on the operation of the equipment but may also entail the preparation of data, the distribution of computer output and network maintenance, and in addition such administrative tasks as file allocation and control.

The operating system is designed to provide information about the computer's performance, including the status of jobs as they progress through the system. This information can be displayed on request on a VDU-type device, known as an *operator's console*, which is generally sited at a central point in the computer room.

Computer operators are responsible for controlling and monitoring activities in the computer room. This includes loading the system after the computer has been down for some reason (i.e. bringing the system back to life), and such tasks as setting up magnetic tapes on tape drives, changing removable disk packs, loading the printer with paper, cleaning tape drives and disks, and various other routine maintenance tasks. The system is designed to monitor its own performance and typically accumulates usage statistics, but operators must be able to recognize unusual behaviour or technical problems within the system and decide on appropriate action. Unusual machine conduct is normally recorded in a log-book as it is observed. As systems become more capable of controlling and monitoring their own activities there is less and less active involvement for operators.

Data has to be input to the system, for example, keying-to-tape or disk, or via a VDU, or data has to be prepared for input to the system. In some installations, particularly those which have many external users, additional staff may be concerned with the control of data. For example, they may be needed to collect data from several branches or departments, or to collect data over variable periods of time, perhaps daily input for weekly/monthly reports, and then to submit the data for processing. This section may also be concerned with the distribution of output to the different departments within an organization, or to external customers, for example, computer generated bills and statements. Responsibility may extend to checking the validity of data and even the accuracy of output. However, an increasing amount of data is captured in computer-usable form at source and results may also be transmitted electronically over networks to the points at which they are needed; thus, staff levels in data preparation are in decline.

In installations where large quantities of data need to be retained, there may be a *file librarian* who is concerned with classifying and cataloguing the various files according to their contents and use, and also with the physical storage of the many reels of magnetic tape (or removable disk packs) which would be required in such an installation.

There may also be a *network controller* who is responsible for setting up and maintaining any local area networks that are needed, for connecting devices to the networks, for monitoring network traffic, and for connections to networks in the outside world. These activities may require the services of a network support team.

The operating group of a computer installation usually operates at least two shifts per day together with some weekend work. An installation may even work twenty-four hours a day, seven days a week, in order to provide the service that is required. The expense of a large computer system may be such that the system is only viable if it operates as near capacity as possible. An installation may be configured such that human operators are not always required in the computer room when the system is running, for example, a system based on disk storage which accepts only input keyed in at remote devices and requires output only to be displayed or printed remotely. Systems which are installed to handle a specific application (non-DP) may even perform without formal operations staff involvement.

The *operations manager* will need to organize the necessary staff and to schedule the workload. He will need to consider job priority and special computing requirements. For example, the payroll program must never be allowed to run late, and a program which requires the line printer for a lengthy period of time (very heavy output) may have to be run at off-peak hours or during the night. However tight the work schedule may be, time must also be set aside for the regular maintenance of equipment, particularly the major maintenance which will normally be handled by engineers from the computer manufacturer.

The organization and deployment of personnel within a DP department will be determined by the amount and type of work that it handles or plans to handle, by the variation of computing equipment in use and proposed, and by the range of computing power that may be available now and in the future. The overall responsibility for the department will rest in the hands of the *data processing manager*.

The DP manager will be involved in the planning and implementation of new projects as well as in controlling existing systems. He will need to work closely with other departments which will be affected. He will draw up procedural methods and standards for the guidance of his staff, and he will oversee their recruitment, training and welfare. He will also be concerned with security, not only of the installation itself, but also the security and control of the libraries of data and program files of all users.

A data processing department may be small or large. In a small department, personnel may have several duties, even to the extent of the manager being involved in systems analysis, writing programs and operating the computer. Irrespective of a department's size, the data processing manager will need to be a businessman as well as a computer expert. He will be concerned with budgets, personnel and equipment. He must be alert to the current needs of the department's users, his clients, and keep himself up-to-date on developments in software and hardware so that he can maintain, and hopefully improve, the high level of efficiency which is required of a DP department.

The use of computers involves a heavy and continuing investment in money, time and skills. A computer system, therefore, should be both *efficient* and *reliable*. A breakdown could entail not merely widespread inconvenience and discomfort, but in some cases it could be a matter affecting life and death, for example, in air traffic control and in certain medical applications. As we have seen in Chapter Nine, such systems would have back-up facilities to ensure continuity of service. However, it is important in *all* systems that emergency procedures be set up, understood and strictly followed by everyone concerned. System faults need to be corrected promptly and, where possible, a system should be designed so that a fault in one piece of equipment does not necessarily mean the stoppage of the entire installation.

Computing will usually be a corporate undertaking requiring a disciplined and well-ordered approach from the design stage through to successful completion of a project.

INFORMATION CENTRES

Initially, the DP department handled the entire computing needs of an organization but as a direct result of involving end users of computers in the development of their own applications, computing gradually spread to other departments. This involvement increased dramatically in the 1980s following the introduction of low cost, easy to use microcomputers and the availability of a wealth of practical, general purpose software (particularly business packages and word processing).

Supporting the individual needs of users spread across different departments is not a role for which the DP department is equipped and it is not a brief which can be absorbed easily. In particular, a typical DP department experienced in mainframe computing and large scale applications is not geared to provide specialist microcomputer technical support. Also, encouraging users to take actual responsibility for their own applications is in conflict with the established practice of centralized corporate control as exemplified by a DP department. Thus in many organizations separate support centres are being set up, known as *information centres*.

The principal role of the information centre is to support any staff outside the DP department who use computers directly. The services provided vary according to the applications involved and the number of people requiring support; however, the emphasis is normally on generating sufficient knowledge in the departments for users to be in a position to help each other. Given the rapid increase in the number of people using computers (office automation as well as specific applications) this is often the only practical approach.

User awareness is stimulated largely through education, and the skills which are needed to use specific packages and build applications are developed through training courses. Consultancy, evaluation of software and equipment maintenance are other services which may be provided by an information centre. Also, there is growing emphasis on the provision of Data Management Systems (DMS). These systems are tailored for use by non-computing personnel featuring special query type languages that are easy to learn. DMS enable organizations to exploit more fully the information at their disposal, aiding decision making and improving efficiency through the knowledge gained from the immediacy and wider dissemination of the information. Typically these systems can relate to financial modelling, graphics or other special software to provide fully integrated information systems.

The information centre is staffed by a mixture of end users with experience of the business who have become experts in specific application areas including the use of specific packages, and specialists in such areas as microcomputers and networks. At the management level, business experience is likely to be considered of greater significance than computing background.

3

The Social Issues

We have seen that computers can be used to store, up-date and analyse information, to direct and control industrial processes, and to aid and encourage scientific research. These, and many other applications, have brought about many changes in the organization and quality of life which affect us directly as individuals or indirectly as members of society. There has been little time in which to adjust to these changes and more time will need to pass before a full appraisal of the impact of computerization on different aspects of life can be made. To complicate matters, the speed of change is accelerating and the changes that are to come may be even more radical than those we have already experienced.

Whatever the use to which computers are applied, there is always a social implication. Whether the computer is used as a clerk to prepare bills, as an information system to provide medical records or judgements on credit-worthiness, in the control of traffic or industrial processes, in management, education or design, or in scientific research and analysis, there are issues involving *people* and such emotive words as automation, redundancy, privacy, security, impersonalization and individuality come to the fore.

INFORMATION PROCESSING

Speedy and efficient information processing is crucial to our socially conscious and highly developed technological society. Computers have helped to reduce the intolerable burden of handling the ever-increasing amount of information with which government departments, public services and business concerns are expected to contend. Having eased

155

the problem, computers, because of their ability to analyse information as well as to retain, up-date and reproduce it, and because of their versatility to present it in a variety of forms, have exacerbated the information explosion and we could not cope with today's volume of information without them.

The availability of information on the scale that computers have made possible has brought many positive benefits. In law or in medicine, for example, access to a mass of information, which it is only possible to search through or analyse quickly enough with the aid of a computer, may benefit clients and patients. In addition, information from the past relating to many other subjects can now be gathered together and used for predicting future patterns so that more reliable decisions of future behaviour can be made in many areas, whether scientific or sociological, private or public.

EFFICIENCY AND PRODUCTIVITY

If we equate the efficiency of a process in terms of its cost, speed and the precision with which it is executed, there is ample evidence in industrial applications that the introduction of the computer has brought positive results. In process control, the use of the computer generally leads to increased efficiency in terms of minimizing wastage and/or raising the quality of output (paper mills, steel) which more than compensates for what may indeed be very high computing costs. It may also raise the safety level of a process (chemical plants), a benefit which is beyond measure in terms of money.

There are applications in which time is critical, apart from considerations of cost and safety. In the design of a large engineering project, such as a power station or dam, many interrelated factors have to be taken into account, the assessment of which involves very many lengthy calculations. This would require many people working over many months and, because of the wide possibilities for human error, experimental models would have to be built, tested, and modified – a costly, slow process. By the time the right answer had been found, the project may be too late or out-of-date. It may have become uneconomic because of rising costs during the lengthy design period. With computers, it is possible to create mathematical models which can simulate the actual and likely conditions, so that the problems can be solved quickly and economically enough so that the implementation of a project is practicable.

In business and commerce, the efficiency claim is well founded. A large part of business operations involves non-creative, routine clerical tasks and the computer can handle a great volume of such tasks more quickly, more accurately and more reliably than is possible manually.

Organizations, large or small, do not thrive or fail because of the presence or absence of a computer, but because of the quality of the people who run them. The larger an organization, the more likely it is to be heavily dependent on computers. Effective computer links between head office, local branches and allied companies have several advantages. The local branch or allied company gains access to a wider range of opportunities, it can buy and sell more economically, offer additional services or better terms and, generally, become more efficient and competitive. Customers appreciate this, but the competing small shop on the corner or local family business will feel itself jeopardized by the remote giant. At head office the computer makes it easier to centralize control and to explore even larger, new horizons. This can lead to streamlining and greater efficiency on the one hand but, on the other, it can lead to a loss of consideration for the individual and for local needs.

The computer can provide many advantages but we must ensure that those advantages are not abused. Any computer system must be so conceived and operated that it is man who runs the machine and can adapt it to his changing needs. The machine cannot be allowed to determine the patterns of our lives, and those of us who enjoy its benefits automatically acquire the responsibility for ensuring that it is used as wisely and as humanely as possible.

AUTOMATION

The object of introducing a computer, or of extending existing computer facilities, may be to increase productivity, to attain a consistently high quality of product, to improve a service and/or to gain knowledge. It may be to extend an existing manual system, perhaps to increase the speed and efficiency of operation, or to handle more work without increasing staff or accommodation, or to provide management with information more quickly.

In most cases, it will also be hoped to keep current and future costs down. Computers and computing, expensive though they often are to install and run, can in many cases achieve these goals. In the process they can eliminate a lot of drudgery – but also jobs. In the majority of applications computers are a long way from ever replacing human judgement. By eliminating drudgery they provide people with the opportunity to pursue more creative endeavours and the exercise of values that are peculiarly human. However, those who fear, rightly or wrongly, that they are likely to lose their jobs because of computers are naturally sceptical of the advantages of computerization.

In business and commerce the computer has complemented rather than replaced the workforce. However, because of the many tasks involved in the collection and handling of information, and the wider use made of more and more information, many jobs have been re-created in other areas. In industrial situations, the computer has taken over many routine, semi-skilled jobs, some of which were also hazardous, and it has offered in their place the possibility of more rewarding jobs. But, in whatever environment, the new jobs are likely to be fewer in number and more technical in nature than those which have been replaced. The use of computer technology has also helped to create new products and services, and hence new jobs. The re-training of personnel for the new, more highly skilled jobs, or for jobs in another industry, is a very important issue. It requires planning and a willingness from those people involved to learn and to adapt.

Computerization has, in many cases, significantly altered work patterns and in so doing has caused some job losses and seems destined to bring about more radical changes in the future. Jobs are likely to be squeezed more as word processing, data base management systems and electronic mail activities merge to bring a high degree of automation to the office and also as uses for *industrial robots* grow.

Industrial robots are programmable devices designed to manipulate tools, to transport parts and perform manufacturing tasks. A robot can be taught by guiding it through its intended role just once in so-called 'teach and learn' mode, or its movements and actions directly controlled by a computer program in real time. At present, tasks are essentially limited to those which can be defined as a precise sequence of steps, e.g. on automated car assembly lines where robots carry out the same assignment on each vehicle as it rolls by. Intelligent robots are anticipated in the future which will be equipped with some measure of visual perception. Rather than pursuing the same sequence of steps these devices will be capable of determining their own course of action once given objectives to meet.

PRIVACY AND INDIVIDUALITY

Data processing has expanded the amount of information (present and past) which is available. We can make use of this in more efficient, productive and automated ways, but what is the implication for the person who is providing the basic information on which these processes are taking place?

Whilst there may be administrative, and even social, advantages in compiling and retaining computer files relating to such things as employment details, tax payments, education, health records, bank accounts and credit-worthiness, such files may contain facts which, as individuals, we consider very sensitive. It is important that this personal information is handled with care and is not available to those who do not require it. If computer systems are correctly designed, unsolicited access to information is theoretically prevented.

As long as the files remain available only to those immediately concerned, all seems fairly reasonable. What is unpalatable is the thought of centralized files in large data banks being cross-referenced to create detailed, individual dossiers. It is the idea of the drawing together of information from different sources which is the crux of the privacy problem. It gives rise to the fear of the machine being used, or abused, for purposes of surveillance.

Whilst it can be argued that, for reasons of efficiency, convenience and economy, information systems *should* be combined and shared, equal consideration should be given to ensure that such action does not lead to an infringement of individual privacy. As data banks become filled with more and more valuable and confidential information, fears about data security and concern for the rights of the individual grow. It is not only the protection of personal data which is the issue but the rights of the individual to have access to the data and to correct or erase erroneous information.

The privacy issues have now been faced by government. The Data Protection Act received royal assent in July 1984. The Act relates to two types of individual: those who compile and maintain data files of personal information on computers (the data users) and those who are the subject of the data files (the data subjects). The purpose of the Act is *not* to prevent the processing of personal data but to *protect* the subjects of that personal data. The Act stipulates that all data users register the existence of all their data files which contain personal information[1] with the Data Protection Registrar. They must also adhere to certain principles in the collection and retention of the information. In addition, part of the Act establishes the right of data subjects to be given access to the personal data held about them.

SECURITY

Computer users themselves have a similar concern that their data banks are not made available to, or can be damaged by, unauthorized persons. Trade and defence secrets must be protected (like individual medical and pay records) against unwarranted exposure and, indeed, sabotage by actual or potential rivals or mischief makers. The threat to security of information, and the threat to individual privacy, are counter arguments for making information systems too widely interchangeable. But if security and privacy are valuable, they are, in computing as elsewhere, qualities which are expensive to achieve and they require continuous maintenance.

Laws for the protection of information and of privacy have been in existence since before the days of computers. The 1984 Act takes computers into consideration. The recent and growing information explosion requires government, and the public at large, to extend its vigilance so that laws, checks and controls are established as necessary for the continued protection of all.

Although we have become very dependent on computers, they are very vulnerable. We have to make sure that the computers themselves are protected so that they can provide the benefits, the power and the knowledge which they offer us. Their security is our security.

CONCLUSIONS AND THE FUTURE

Society is already more computerized than many people may imagine and because of the implications of this, some of which we have examined, it is clearly important that people become aware of the potentialities so that they can seek to influence future use. Awareness hinges on education and this is growing and should continue to expand – hopefully at the same fast pace at which the youthful, vigorous computer industry is itself expanding.

In the final analysis, man is shaped by his own tools. What of the motor car? Many benefits have undoubtedly been derived from this invention, but the consequences wrought on society have been far reaching, and they were unforeseeable in the first instance. The increased mobility provided by the automobile has helped to alter the very structure of family life. Roads and motorways have scarred the face of the land, and increasing traffic accidents and pollution have brought suffering to motorists and non-motorists alike.

Inevitably, the computer seems destined to bring about radical changes and some of these we may not yet have appreciated as potentially problematic. The goal, surely, is not to create a better world of computers, but to create a better world for man to live in. There may be conflict in balancing 'progress' with 'civilization' and, in the long run, society can only blame itself if computers are allowed to create more problems than they solve. What is happening to the under-developed countries? Are computers helping to close, or to widen, the gap between those who have and those who have not? In China, for example, it is expected that computers and semiconductor technology will play a leading role in helping to transform the country into a modern advanced technological society.

The Industrial Revolution saw many technological developments, the social effects of which have changed over several generations before becoming absorbed into our way of life. Significant changes have taken place in the thirty-five years or so since the computer industry came into being, but several lifetimes may have to pass before the social and cultural effects of the computer are fully understood.

What of tomorrow's world? The advance of the micro-electronics industry has provided a new impetus to an already rapidly moving computer industry. Computing power will become even cheaper, computers will be easier to handle and become even more widely available to the general public. This will affect our lives as individuals and the societies in which we live.

Computers are pointing the way to an automated society. The development of robots to work in certain hostile situations, such as fire fighting, mines, security of sensitive establishments and space exploration, could bring considerable benefits. Industrial robots, which have the capacity to change industrial practice radically and to bring about automation on a scale not yet envisaged or understood, may not be so socially acceptable. If industry is to remain competitive robots will inevitably be used in increasing numbers on the factory shop floor and on assembly lines. Some industrial countries have already cut their production costs considerably by their investment in robots. Society will have to decide on the balance that needs to be struck between the use of robots and the gainful employment of people. The market for goods produced by robots cannot remain buoyant if purchasing power is substantially reduced through widespread unemployment or under-employment. The sight of microprocessor controlled robots assembling cars is a dramatic example of factory automation. Less dramatic, but also far reaching in its consequences to society, is the development of the electronic office and consequent reorganization of office practice.

The use of the computer as an information provider within the home is only just beginning to be exploited. Whenever fully accepted and established, this method of communication has quite a profound effect on life. Access to computer-stored information is already possible through viewdata and teletext systems but usage is growing more slowly than first anticipated. The cost of viewdata for access to what is essentially passive information is currently too high for the domestic scene. In consequence, there has been a change of emphasis in the technology for the development and support of in-house viewdata systems for business and British Telecom has introduced a Gateway service which allows private databases to be linked into the public service. Most in-house viewdata systems are used as an alternative to telephone or personal contact. It is expected that the emphasis in viewdata will shift from information retrieval and exchange to transaction applications in which something is looked up and then acted upon. With more tangible benefits to offer from the home, like shopping and banking, it is expected that domestic use will begin to flourish. In addition, when the speed of viewdata is increased through the development of wider bandwidth communication links, there will be virtually no limit to the technology. The true significance of a universally available information service which can be used without any prior knowledge of computers and without any training is difficult to assess. It has the potential to be the most powerful and useful information retrieval system so far invented.

New technology now coming out of university research laboratories is beginning to change the image of a computer from an exceedingly fast calculating device to a machine which is capable of mimicking human thought processes. Computers with the capabilities to reason, make judgements and learn are on the horizon. Already, computer systems displaying some degree of 'artificial intelligence' exist and are used to perform tasks once thought to be the sole province of *homo sapiens* such as diagnosing lung diseases, locating mineral deposits and siting oil wells.

The world stands on the threshold of a second computer age. Experts are convinced it is only a question of time before 'thinking' computers open up a whole new range of applications in the office, the factory, in medical and military areas, and also in the home. Artificial intelligence (AI) has the potential to change our way of life. However, there are many technical hardware and software problems still to be overcome before the introduction of what is already being referred to as the fifth generation of computers, that is, the family of machines designed specifically for applications requiring the attribute of artificial intelligence.

Data processing is based on processing information whereas artificial intelligence is concerned with processing ideas and knowledge. A factor which inhibits the development of AI is the issue of knowledge representation. Exactly how do you express knowledge in a simple enough form for the computer to handle it? In addition, traditional programming methods do not encourage the processing of ideas and knowledge. The key to AI lies with new style programming and software. The new software seeks to emulate the performance of the human brain. At concept level it attempts to do this by making a series of fuzzy estimates which are gradually refined by skipping across logical patterns until an acceptable judgement or decision is reached.

AI has been applied with varying degrees of success in a number of areas including game playing, natural language recognition and expert systems. Chess is an example of game playing. The game demands intelligence and skill from players; however, the moves of the game are easy enough to represent on a computer – hence its suitability for computerization.[2] The significance of game playing is that the methods used can be usefully applied to other areas of AI.

Computers cannot yet completely interpret continuous English text (or any other language for that matter) but they can deal with certain words and phrases, and even longer passages when the subject matter is specific. Natural languages are structured according to rules of syntax but the rules are complex and subject to exceptions, and thus difficult to master. In addition, there is the issue of grasping the meaning of words within the context that they are used before the passage can be fully understood.

The development and application of artificial intelligence has also enabled the creation of so-called expert systems. The purpose of an expert system is to provide reasoned advice in a particular field and at a level commensurate with that which a human expert would provide. An expert system comprises a knowledge base (carefully structured to permit optimum use) and a set of rules for manipulating the knowledge. Some systems are able to learn through experience and thus build on the knowledge with which they were initially endowed. Other systems operate using knowledge fixed at the time the base is constructed. In both cases the body of knowledge is derived from the understanding and wisdom of human experts. It may contain vague and incomplete knowledge in addition to hard facts, just as the human mind does.

Expert systems are expected to become more sophisticated and widely used in the 1990s assuming the advent of fifth generation computers (see below). At present there are examples of expert systems in use in the field of medicine – in diagnosis, treatment planning and the monitoring of experiments. Other applications include geological prospecting and the provision of legal advice. The advantage of an expert system is that, in providing reasoned advice, the system will always sift through all available knowledge in a logical and systematic way. Nothing is ignored. However, an expert system is only as good as the wealth of knowledge in the base and the correctness of the program design. Most of today's systems are used to support and supplement human judgement rather than to supplant it.

In October 1981, Japan announced a new initiative aimed at developing a new generation of computers (the fifth generation) that would incorporate a high level of artificial intelligence. The development path is expected to extend well into the 1990s. Other countries quickly followed suit and set up their own development programmes.

The fifth generation is to solve complex problems which demand expertise and powers of reasoning when tackled by humans. Use is expected to be made of subsets of natural languages for interfacing (communicating) with the systems so that they can be used quite naturally by people who are not necessarily computer experts.

A fifth generation computer will be different in design from the computer of today. It will contain a large number of processors, rather than a single processor, and these will be arranged in three major groupings: a *knowledge base system*, an *inference mechanism* and an *intelligent user interface*. The knowledge base system is to house a very large store of knowledge in a very carefully structured form to suit the requirements of the inference mechanism which is designed to reach conclusions using the knowledge base. The aim of the intelligent user interface is to provide the user with a way of working which is close to the human thought process and not tied to the way the computer functions. With today's computer at the interface level the user has to learn to think like a computer but with tomorrow's system (the fifth generation) the aim is that the computer will think as a user does.

There are five major research and development programmes under-way in the quest to develop fifth generation computers: the Icot programme (Japan), Darpa and MCC (USA), Esprit (EEC) and Alvey (UK). These programmes are separate initiatives with separate goals but a measure of collaboration does now exist. The Alvey programme, which is 50% state funded, is pursuing research in four principal areas: software engineering, VLSI chip architecture,[3] intelligent knowledge-based systems and intelligent user interfaces.

Methods used for the development of computer software are continually evolving. The increasing length and complexity of software, and the cost of producing it, is forcing a reassessment of traditional programming practice (inclusive of systems analysis). In addition, the particular requirements of software for the fifth generation, with its emphasis on the use of artificial intelligence in programming, is accelerating the change. Software engineering is the name of the new approach. Software engineering sets great store on program design and structure, and on the correctness of software and standard of performance. It is carried out by teams of skilled people who need knowledge of formal mathematics and logic, and computer science as well as skills in the use of a particular programming language. Software engineering also demands special management skills.

It is too soon to be specific about future applications but it seems certain that many fields of human endeavour will become more dependent on computers and this will inevitably lead to a widening of horizons which were previously unimaginable. Satellites have made the world smaller. A space shot recorded snow patterns of the Himalayas and it is said that this could be invaluable in the development of large-scale irrigation schemes of incalculable benefit to the arid regions of the sub-continent of India. The real significance is that we are on the threshold of new discoveries and new worlds previously beyond man's comprehension.

NOTES

1 By far the biggest consumer of personal information is the government itself. It runs hundreds of computers containing millions of personal files. Some of this information may be considered of no consequence in terms of sensitivity – the fact that you own a car. Other information may be seen as highly sensitive – police records for example. However, whatever we think about it, computers are now the standard way of retaining information of a personal nature. We all become the subject of a computer file within hours of being alive.

2 The computer has 'mastered' the game. Software can be obtained at different levels of suitability, from beginning players to skilled practitioners.

3 VLSI (Very Large Scale Integration). There are chips today which contain hundreds of thousands of elements. This is insufficient for the needs of fifth generation computers which will be constructed from large numbers of VLSI chips, each containing millions of elements.

APPENDICES

1

The Development
of Computers

The computer evolved as a result of man's search for fast, accurate calculating devices. However, the birth of computers depended upon many other factors, such as the acceleration of certain technological improvements from the early 1900s, the availability of vast sums of money for computer development as a result of World War II, changes in government attitudes, and the evolution of basic computing theories as developed by von Neumann,[1] Shannon[2] and Turing.[3] It is hoped that this Appendix will be of interest for its own sake as well as affording a background knowledge of the development of computers. Essentially, there are three kinds of calculating devices: manual, mechanical and automatic.

Manual devices include the abacus, in evidence in the Tigris-Euphrates Valley c. 3500 BC, and John Napier's bone or cardboard multiplication calculator designed in the early 17th century. It is interesting to note that adapted versions of Napier's invention were still being manufactured in 1888 and in the Far East the abacus was still in use in the 1970s.

Mechanical devices include Blaise Pascal's adding machine (1642) and Gottfried Wilhelm von Leibnitz's stepped calculator (1694). It was not until the early 19th century that the principles of these machines were used with any commercial success. They have changed little since that period. It was left to the genius of Charles Babbage, born in Totnes, Devonshire in 1791, to design a machine which was to be the forerunner of the electronic computer as we know it today. The Analytical Engine has already been discussed in detail in Chapter One where it was remarked that precision engineering required to manufacture the machine was not available in Babbage's day.

Many years were to pass before Babbage's dream was realized.

During the late 19th and early 20th centuries, a great deal of activity took place in the field of punched-card tabulating systems. We shall investigate this briefly since it has a direct bearing upon the development of the computer industry.

TABULATING MACHINES

Following the 1880 population census, the United States Census Bureau realized that, with the growth in population, its existing methods of tabulating and analysing the ten-yearly US National Census had become totally inadequate. Herman Hollerith, born in 1860, devised a system based on the principle of punching holes onto cards, similar to Jacquard's idea. As a result of a competition held between Hollerith's system and two rival (non-mechanized) systems, he gained a contract to supply his equipment for the 1890 census. It involved the punching of 56 million cards, and his system proved to be a great success. International interest was quickly aroused and the punched card system emerged.

Austria used the system for its December 1890 Census. The New York Central Railroad were the first to attempt a commercial application by using the system for office accounting as early as 1895. For this particular application, Hollerith had to provide a tabulator with the ability to add rather than merely count, and he based its design on an electromagnetic version of the Leibnitz stepped wheel.

In 1896, Hollerith formed his own company, the Tabulating Machine Company, which he sold in 1911. It merged with two other companies to form the Computing-Tabulating-Recording Company. By 1924, this company became the International Business Machines Corporation (better known now as IBM), the largest manufacturer, even today, of punched card equipment.

During the years between 1920 and 1930, the punched card system developed steadily, not only in the States but also in Britain and Europe. One of the earliest applications in the UK was in the field of astronomy. It concerned the work of Dr L.J. Comrie of the British Nautical Almanac Office, who in 1926 computed the future positions of the moon at twelve hourly intervals for the period 1935–2000. This he did using a Burroughs Accounting Machine in conjunction with Hollerith punched cards. It was estimated that half a million cards were used in his mammoth calculation.

PUNCHED CARDS AND PAPER TAPE

Card punching and reading

Punched card input was once the traditional form of communicating with computers but today there are relatively few applications in which the punched card is still used. More direct and convenient methods have evolved and are preferred, for example the terminal keyboard.

As early as 1801, Joseph Jacquard built a weaving loom in which the movement of the threads was controlled by the presence and absence of holes in cards. The standard punched card used with computers developed directly from an idea patented by Herman Hollerith in 1889. A standard card was divided into 80 columns and 12 rows. Only one character could be represented in any of the 80 columns, this providing a maximum of 80 characters per card.

A character was represented by punching one, two or three holes in any one column. This is illustrated in figure A1.1. Holes were punched into a blank card by a punch machine whose keyboard resembled that of a typewriter. By typing a character at the keyboard, a set of holes would be punched into one column.

A card reader provides the interface between the punched card and the computer. The reader is designed to accept the code and to generate electronic pulses, representing sequences of bits which the computer can understand. Each card passes between a light source and a set of photo-electric cells. The presence of a hole causes the light to create a pulse by triggering one of the cells. Some card readers can operate at speeds up to 2000 cards per minute.[4] This may be considered fast for a mechanical device in which the physical movement of cards is involved, but it is very slow compared with the speed that the CPU can transfer information internally.

Paper tape

Another common medium for communicating with the computer was paper tape. It had been in use for many years before the invention of the computer. It can be found on old pianola rolls and was (and, to some extent, still is) used by typesetters (the Monotype process). The computing industry has adopted, and adapted, this technique. Computer tape is normally 1 inch wide, comes in rolls, and may be used in any length up to several hundred feet. Information is recorded as holes

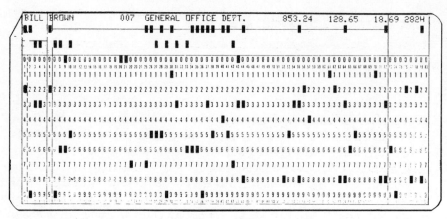

Figure A1.1

punched in rows across the width of the tape, with one row representing one character. The maximum number of holes in this row is referred to as the number of *channels* on the tape. An eight-channel tape is the most common. Tapes make use of different codes depending on the number of channels.

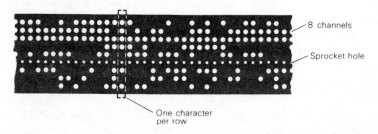

8 channels

Sprocket hole

One character
per row

Figure A1.2 Punched tape – eight-channel tape. The sprocket holes run the length of the tape for the purpose of feeding the tape through the tape punching and reading device.

The paper tape reader operates in a similar manner to the card reader. The tape passes a reading unit where the presence or absence of holes is sensed and converted to electrical pulses. A speed of 2000 characters per second is considered a high transfer rate with typical speeds less than half this rate.

Paper tape, like punched cards, is not now so widely used. Certain teletypewriter terminals (see page 40) may use paper tape to record the input of data or program results. Similarly, paper tape attachments for recording data are associated with a number of business machines, e.g. various accounting type machines and cash registers.

THE ADVENT OF DIGITAL COMPUTERS

Harvard Mark I

In 1937, Howard A. Aiken of Harvard University, using the techniques already developed for punched card machinery, began work on the design of a fully automatic calculating machine in collaboration with the International Business Machines Corporation. His aim was to develop a machine which would help him in the solution of complex differential equations, the vast calculations of which would have been impractical manually.

Seven years later, in May 1944, the designs became a reality. In August of the same year, the now historically famous Harvard Mark I was donated to Harvard University in Cambridge, Massachusetts where it was initially used for classified work for the US Navy.

It had taken technology over a century to catch up with the ideas first mooted by Charles Babbage in Cambridge, England in 1833, but once having achieved this, a phenomenal rate of development followed. Much of value was gained from the research surrounding a project mounted on such a lavish scale as the Mark I. Significantly, the machine proved to be extremely reliable and it remained in active use at Harvard for fifteen years.

The Mark I, or Automatic Sequence Controlled Calculator as it was sometimes called, was complex in design and huge in size. Physically, the machine measured fifty-one feet in length and eight feet in height. It is said to have contained three-quarters of a million parts and in construction to have used more than five hundred miles of wire. It was capable of performing five basic operations; addition, subtraction, multiplication, division and table reference. It was extremely slow by present-day standards but, nevertheless, its realization represented a remarkable achievement. The addition of two numbers took 0.3 of a second and multiplication 4.5 seconds. The magnitude of a number was restricted to twenty-three decimal digits.

The store of the machine consisted of a number of registers each of which was made up of a number of counter wheels. Operating instructions were fed to the computer, not via punched cards, but on punched tape. Each instruction was divisible into two parts; that which specified the type of operation, and that which indicated the storage location where the number to be operated upon was to be found and re-stored in its new form. Information for processing (data) was fed to the machine chiefly by way of punched cards, though values could also be entered by depressing switches manually. Results from processing appeared in punched card form or were typed by an electric typewriter. The Mark I was really an electro-mechanical machine in that its CPU depended on both mechanical and electronic devices for its operation.

ENIAC

The innovation of very high speed vacuum tube switching devices led to the first all-electronic computer, the Electronic Numerical Integrator and Calculator, formally dedicated on 15 February 1946, only two years after the Mark I. ENIAC was constructed at the Moore School of Engineering of the University of Pennsylvania by a design team led by Professors Eckert and Mauchly.

Achievements were most impressive. In a single hour ENIAC could accomplish calculations which would have taken Mark I one week to perform. The addition of two numbers was achieved in 200 microseconds, and multiplication in 2,800 microseconds.

The machine was small in terms of storage capacity and, as it was designed for a specific purpose (ballistics), its use was limited. However, whatever the shortcomings of ENIAC, it was represented an impressive feat of electronic engineering.

Von Neumann

Before the completion of ENIAC, a significant event occurred. This was the publication of a paper – 'Theory and Techniques of Electronic Digital Computers' by Dr John von Neumann,[5] a consultant to the ENIAC project. The paper represented the first attempt to analyse the problem of computer design in logical terms and it undoubtedly had an enormous impact, for it has since influenced considerably the development of the modern digital computer. Von Neumann's most significant concept was that of the *stored* program. This embodied the idea that a sequence of instructions might be held in the *store* of the computer for the purpose of directing the flow of operations, and that these instructions themselves might then be altered and manipulated in much the same way as data. EDVAC, the Electronic Discrete Variable Automatic Computer, was to be such a machine.

EDVAC

EDVAC made use of acoustic delay lines consisting of tanks of mercury in which the trains of pulses representing data circulated and re-circulated until required to be operated upon by the arithmetic unit. Both the instructions and the numbers to be used for calculation were stored in the memory unit.

There were engineering difficulties during the development stage, some, no doubt, attributable to the departure of Eckert and Mauchly who left to form their own computer manufacturing company.[6] In the end, EDVAC was not the first practical computer to operate with an internally stored program. This distinction fell to the British development, EDSAC.

Manchester Mark I

The earliest stored program computer to operate was probably the small experimental machine built at Manchester University and is generally claimed to have run its first program in June 1948. Its storage capacity, only 32 words, each of 31 binary digits to store data, instructions and working, was too limited to be of any practical use.

The Manchester project was set up by Professor M. H. A. Newman, aided by I. J. Good, F. C. Williams and T. Kilburn. As the latter two claim in a paper, the machine 'was built primarily to test the soundness of the storage principle employed (i.e. the Williams-tube type of electrostatic store) and to permit experience to be gained with this type of machine before embarking on the design of a full-size machine'. Brian Randell points out[7] part of the interest in the Manchester project is that it does not apparently descend solely from the work at the Moore School.

EDSAC

Work on EDSAC, the Electronic Delay Storage Automatic Calculator, was started early in 1947, in the Cambridge University Mathematical

Laboratory by a team under the leadership of Professor Maurice Wilkes who had previously spent some time in the States with the EDVAC team. The machine executed its first program in May 1949. It employed a mercury delay line storage system with an access time of one millisecond. Addition was accomplished in 1500 microseconds, and multiplication in 4000 microseconds. The electronic, stored-program, digital computer, as we know it today, had arrived!

COMPUTER 'GENERATIONS'

There is no clear cut pattern of development after EDSAC emerged. The history is tied up in a tangle of technological advances, university research and company amalgamations. What is evident is that the computer industry, as such, did not establish itself until a good deal of the problems had been ironed out on the early prototype projects, and until improvements in components made it cost-effective to produce machines for general use and, also, until industry, commerce and government departments recognized the value of using computers.

In order to simplify matters and at the same time provide a framework for the growth of the computer industry, we shall look at the so-called 'generations' of computers. The custom of referring to the computer era in terms of generations came into wide use after 1964. Although there is a certain amount of overlapping between generations, the approximate dates shown in figure A1.3 are generally accepted. Originally, the term *generation* was used to distinguish between varying hardware technologies. Since 1968, it has been extended to include both the hardware and the software, which together make up an entire system.

The first generation of computers was marked by the use of vacuum tubes for the electronic components and by the use of either electrostatic tubes (CRT) or mercury delay lines for storage. Examples of such first generation machines are EDSAC (operational in 1949), SEAC (1950, the first stored program computer operational in the US), EDVAC (1951) and IAS (1952).

The second generation machines were initially marked by either magnetic drum or magnetic core storage and, later, by the use of the transistor in place of vacuum tubes.

Under the joint sponsorship of the US Air Force and office of Naval Research, WHIRLWIND I was designed and developed between 1947 and 1951 at the Massachusetts Institute of Technology. It used a cathode ray tube store, but this was replaced in 1952 by the first successful use of

GENERATION	ELECTRONIC COMPONENT	ADVANTAGES	DISADVANTAGES	COMMENTS
1st generation 1940—52	Vacuum tubes	Vacuum tubes were the only electronic components available	Large-size Generated heat Air-conditioning required Unreliable Constant maintenance	Manual assembly of individual components into a functioning unit
2nd generation 1952—64	Transistors	Smaller-size Less heat generated More reliable Faster	Air-conditioning required Maintenance	As above
3rd generation 1964—71	Integrated circuits	Even smaller size Even lower heat generation Less power required Even more reliable Faster still	Initially, problems with manufacture	Less human labour at assembly stage
4th generation 1971—	Large-scale integrated circuits	No air-conditioning Minimal maintenance High component density Cheapest		As above

Figure A1.3 Generation chart of electronic components

a magnetic core memory. The attributes of magnetic core are compactness, reliability and speed of access. However, it took another six years before this type of store was widely used by the industry. The IBM 605 provides an example of an early magnetic drum machine which sold far in excess of the original sales estimate (1000 as opposed to 50).

Although the transistor was invented in 1948, several years of development and trial passed before it made any real impact upon the computer industry. The breakthrough came in 1954 when the Philco Corporation developed a transistor which was to lead to high-speed machines as well as ones with increased capacity. Within four years vacuum tubes were obsolete.

The NCR 304, a joint effort between its designers, the National Cash Register, and its builders, General Electric, was the first all-transistorized computer. However, few were sold due to its relatively slow performance and its limited capacity.

With both these generations, however, the basic component was a discrete or separate (individual) entity. The many thousands of separate components had to be assembled by hand into functioning circuits. It was the cost of labour at this assembly stage which became increasingly expensive. In the Harvard Mark I, an electro-mechanical computer, some 500 miles of wire were required to link the various components together – all by hand.

Attempts were made to reduce this assembly stage. The breakthrough came just a few years after the introduction of the transistor but it took almost a decade before the manufacturing techniques for this new microelectronic technology were mastered. Once this happened, it became possible to combine a handful of circuits into an integrated whole on a small surface less than 5 mm square (¼ inch). This new technology was called **integrated circuits** (ICs) and its real impact was in eliminating the labour costs previously required.

It was in 1964 (approximately) that ICs began to be used in any number in the construction of computers, thereby ushering in the third generation. At first, only a handful, about ten, components could be integrated. This became known as a small-scale integration (SSI). As the techniques for manufacturing ICs improved, it became possible to combine up to a hundred components, known as medium-scale integration (MSI).

Eventually, many thousands of components were able to be packed onto the same small area, 5 mm square by 1 mm thick. This became known as large-scale integration (LSI) and has become known as the *fourth generation*. It is LSI technology which has led to the development of the microcomputer. Before .long it is expected that one million components can be packed onto the small silicon chip (or some other base material), known as very-large-scale integration (VLSI). Already, RAM memories of 256+K bytes are available commercially. Even this is not enough. Experts forecast that in time, ten million components will be a practical possibility. But what does all this mean?

Today, the world's largest computer is the CRAY machine. By any standard it is a huge computer comprising 200,000 circuits with thirty components per circuit, that is six million components. What the microelectronic experts are saying is that within the next two decades it will be possible to put 10 million components upon a single chip. In other words, in the future we shall have the pocket size maxi-mainframe. With a few more chips for central memory and voice input and output, current mainframes could shrink to the size of calculators.

If all this seems fanciful, let us consider what has already been achieved. ENIAC, developed at a cost of $500,000 (1946), consisted of 18,000 vacuum tubes and occupied 3000 cubic feet. Yet, less than 30 years later a microprocessor of comparable computing power could be purchased for a mere $10 (1980 – and taking no account of inflation) and is small enough to be sent through the post. If this had been foretold, would the designers of ENIAC have believed it to be possible? It is said that they claimed four ENIACs would be sufficient for the world's needs, and yet within twenty years millions of computers were in existence. If we believe today's experts, all they are saying is that a similar reduction will be technically feasible for current mainframes within the next few decades.

To put these latest computers into perspective, let us compare a Fairchild product, the F8, which allows I/O access to the microcomputer via a VDU and printer, with one of the earliest computers, ENIAC. ENIAC occupied 3000 cubic feet, the F8 takes up 0.011 cubic feet (i.e. some 300,000 times smaller). The F8 consumes 56,000 times *less* power, has a larger main memory; is 10,000 times *more* reliable than ENIAC; weighs 1 lb whereas ENIAC weighed 30 tonnes. These latest computers are comparable to the early ones but are smaller, more reliable, more powerful, but less costly. Where all this will lead the computer industry and, much more important, our society as a whole, it is difficult to predict. In much the same way, a hundred years ago, Alexander Bell could not have predicted the future organization of society as a result of the impact of the telephone upon present-day communications. Certainly, the marriage of computer power, via advances in microtechnology, with telecommunications will have a profound effect upon the society of 2001 AD. Already, we hear about access to many TV channels via satellite communications rather than our limited four channels of today. Viewers will possess the power to select which outcome of a programme they prefer to see, or, to vote upon some referendum from their lounge via a simple input pad linked to a TV centre. Undoubtedly, our society will change, and is changing as a result of the impact of microelectronics upon computers and communications.

NOTES

1 John von Neumann's contribution is discussed later in this appendix.

2 In 1938, Claude Shannon noticed that Boole's algebra (developed in 1845) could be used for describing relay and switching circuits.

3 Alan Turing developed the theory of a machine for solving almost any arithmetical problem. If Turing's theoretical machine could not solve a problem, then no computer, however sophisticated, could solve it.

4 This means a maximum transfer rate of some 2600 characters per second on the basis of a maximum of 80 characters per card.

5 In some sources, the credit for the paper is attributed solely to von Neumann, but it seems likely that Eckert and Mauchly were also deeply involved.

6 Eventually known as UNIVAC.

7 *The Origins of Digital Computers – Selected Papers*: see References.

2
Programming Languages

Programming languages are divided into several categories – there is the machine level, i.e. the binary level which the computer actually executes; there is the assembly level, i.e. a machine-orientated version which allows the use of mnemonics. Both of these are termed *low level* because they mirror directly the machine's architecture.

There are high level languages, also known as problem-orientated languages because they allow the programmer to write instructions more closely related to a class of problem rather than to the constraints of a given computer's architecture.

There is a higher level yet which includes packages, such as word processing, data base management and spreadsheets. These languages allow users to specify the information they want, in non-programming terms, and the package will produce the required results. These are closely related to Fourth Generation Languages (4GLs) where, again, the accent is on specifying *what* is wanted rather than specifying the steps (the procedure) involved in *how* it is done. These languages are non-procedural, therefore, as opposed to the conventional high level languages which are procedural since the programmer writes the steps (instructions) which specify how the task is to be solved.

Many hundreds of programming languages exist and when surveying them, it is commonly accepted to attach a descriptive label to each, e.g. 'scientific', 'commercial'. This can be useful since such classifications aid our understanding. However, such broad classifications should be used with caution. Although Fortran is a scientific language, it has been used quite successfully for commercial payroll programs! Another classification frequently used is related to the environment in which languages are used, e.g. in real-time, batch processing mode. This method also has its limitations since the language could be determined more by an operating system than by any inherent features of the language itself.

However, Figure A2.1 attempts to classify the various high level languages but the reader is advised not to attach a too rigid adherence to the chart. The rest of this appendix discusses briefly some of the more common high level languages.

SCIENTIFIC LANGUAGES

FORTRAN (formula translator)

The first available high-level language was FORTRAN, developed in 1956 for use on an IBM 704 computer. Its prime purpose was to solve mathematical and scientific problems which were allowed to be written in a simple English style with the mathematical expressions stated naturally, e.g. $A = B + C - D$.

During the middle 1960s, it became widely used on a number of machines resulting in a variety of 'dialects', the most important being IBM FORTRAN II and IBM FORTRAN IV. By 1962, the American Standards Institute (ASA) set up a working party to produce a specification for the language. Two versions were finally approved in March 1966, ASA FORTRAN (similar to IBM FORTRAN IV) and ASA BASIC FORTRAN (similar to IBM FORTRAN II). Their popularity grew to such an extent that most manufacturers had to ensure that their dialect of FORTRAN conformed to these standards.

In August 1966, the ASA changed its name to the United States of America Standards Institute (USASI) and this was changed in October 1969 to the American National Standards Institute (ANSI). A new 'standard' FORTRAN, called FORTRAN 77, was defined in 1977. It contains several additional features over and above those in FORTRAN IV, such as character type, improved file handling features and the IFTHENELSE construction to improve program structure.

Work on another version is in progress called FORTRAN 8x. Until this is complete the 'x' is being used, but it is expected to be fully defined in 1988.

ALGOL (algorithmic language)

Like FORTRAN, this language was intended for the solution of numeric and scientific problems, and it differs little in scope from FORTRAN. ALGOL was originally developed in 1958, resulting in ALGOL 58. It was revised in 1960 and the importance of this version (ALGOL 60) lies in the elegance of its structure, something which, historically, will remain long after its demise.

Types of language	Language names	Applications
Commercial	COBOL, COBOL85, CIS-COBOL, RPG/2	Essentially, data processing applications where the emphasis is on files of data rather than numerical computation, e.g., invoicing, stock control.
Scientific	FORTRAN, FORTRAN 77, FORTRAN 8x, ALGOL 60	Used in engineering, scientific and mathematical applications where the emphasis is on 'number crunching'.
General purpose	PL/1, PASCAL, ALGOL 86	Used for either commercial or scientific applications. Extended versions of BASIC also fall into this category.
Interactive	APL, BASIC, LOGO, FORTH	Specially developed for terminal use rather than a batch processing environment.
Real-time	CORAL 66, RTL/2, ADA, MODULA-2, OCCAM	These languages contain modules which must be executed in response to external signals arriving in an unpredictable manner and which must be executed within given time constraints.
Systems programming languages	C, PL/M, PL/Z	These are used for the development of operating systems formerly performed by assembly level languages. C is implemented on a wide range of machines. PL/M was developed for the Intel 8080 microprocessor, PL/Z for the Zilog Z8000.
Artificial intelligence	LISP, PROLOG	AI languages are of increasing interest with the advent of the Japanese fifth generation project. Prolog is the language chosen to support the Japanese Project.

Figure A2.1

The revised ALGOL 60 report introduced into the computing milieu structural concepts, a precision of language definition, and a certain discipline of programming procedures. These features in FORTRAN had, in contrast, been basically simple.

COMMERCIAL LANGUAGES

COBOL (common business oriented language)

An international business language was inspired by the US Department of Defense in order to handle its many everyday commercial problems. COBOL came out around 1958. It attempts to be a subset of English and is meant to be readable by non-programmers. Its data structures, therefore, were devised to facilitate everyday office file procedures.

Unfortunately, COBOL has not lived up to the original expectations and cannot be fully understood by the uninitiated (office managers), and its propensity towards English has turned it into a verbose language (from the programmer's point of view), yet it remains the most widely used commercial language.

ANSI released a new standard – ANSI COBOL 85 which includes many concessions to modern thinking. CIS-COBOL ('Compact, Interactive Standard') is used on personal computers. Later versions also include powerful debugging aids to speed up interactive development of COBOL programs.

RPG (Report Program Generator)

RPG was developed by IBM as a result of customer requests for an easy and economic mechanism for producing reports and was launched in 1961 for use on the IBM 1401 computer. Today, RPG is run on IBM 360/370 series and the System 3 as well as several other makes such as the ICL 2903 and Univac 9000 series.

When System 3 was introduced by IBM, it was announced that it would use RPG II. This latter version retains all the features of RPG but contains some additional features such as the ability to work with arrays.

The term 'report' is used in a broad sense to include the preparation of invoices and cheque payments, as well as 'normal' reports. It was originally developed to help the transfer of punched card accounting systems to computers. The user specifies the format of the files and of the desired report and the system generates a program to do the job. It is a forerunner of 4GLs.

GENERAL PURPOSE LANGUAGES

By 'general purpose' we simply mean languages not specifically designed for commercial or scientific tasks. There are three to consider, PL/1, ALGOL 68 and PASCAL.

PL/1 (programming language 1)

By the early 1960s, a programmer had a choice of languages. For numeric work there was FORTRAN or ALGOL; for systems programming some assembly language would be preferred; COBOL was used for commercial applications, whilst for more specialized applications such as list processing or string manipulation, there was LISP or SNOBOL. Some installations were beginning to find such a plethora somewhat difficult, not only from an educational aspect but also in the support and maintenance of such a large number of language translators. PL/1 was the intended panacea.

PL/1 was developed in the middle of the 1960s in an attempt to combine the features of these earlier languages. The intention was to create a language which would be adequate for programming *any* kind of application. This resulted, of course, in the production of a language which is enormous by any standards and one that is not easy to learn in its totality. Furthermore, it was developed by IBM and its use is often limited to the equipment of this one manufacturer.

Over the past decade, it has not captured the attention originally anticipated. The current trend in language design is not towards the large language but towards smaller and more elegant ones, e.g. APL. The few features which they possess can be combined by the programmer in such a way as to create, in effect, an individual language for each application.

ALGOL 68

This language has been little used. It was defined by a committee of academics (mainly) under the auspices of IFIP. The resulting language was considerably powerful and introduced many new concepts based on sound theoretical principles. However, it is a forbidding language even for practising programmers.

PASCAL

PASCAL (not an acronym, for once, but named after the great Frenchman) is one of those high-level languages which the enthusiast claims is a joy to use. It was originally designed by Nicklaus Wirth in 1968, belongs to the ALGOL stable and the first operational compiler became available in 1970. One of its more important features is to allow the programmer to structure data in *his* way. Standard PASCAL was originally developed and implemented on the CDC 6000 series but has been developed for use on other machines. It is well thought of as a programming language for student teaching and has become a highly popular language especially on micros. The early version of PASCAL used on micros was developed at the University of San Diego and marketed as UCSD-PASCAL. The dominant version today however is Borland's Turbo-PASCAL. As a language, PASCAL is highly acclaimed within the teaching fraternity. The best modern programming techniques can be taught so that highly structured programs can be written.

INTERACTIVE LANGUAGES

Most of the languages mentioned so far were developed for use within a batch processing environment. They can still be used from a terminal and used in an interactive sense. However, two languages were designed especially for interactive use, BASIC and APL.

BASIC (Beginners All-purpose Symbolic Instruction Code)

This is a language designed primarily for use on time-sharing computer systems. To understand an interactive programming language like BASIC it is not necessary to learn complex programming techniques. It is, in fact, intended for those who have no experience with using computers or writing computer programs. BASIC has few grammatical rules and can be said to be user rather than system orientated. It resembles FORTRAN in many respects, making use of standard mathematical notation, but serves business applications equally well. It can be learnt in a few hours, concentrated study and, though simple, it is flexible and reasonably powerful. The language was developed by Professor John Kemeny and Thomas Kurtz in the mid-sixties at Dartmouth College in the United States for use on a time-sharing system. Because of its simplicity and bias towards the user, it is a language well suited for use in education and has become extremely popular with microcomputer users.

APL (A Programming Language)

APL, designed for time-sharing, is derived from the formal mathematical notation invented in 1962 by Kenneth E. Iverson. The APL system, known as APL/360, was developed by Iverson together with Adin D. Falkoff, Larry M. Breed and staff of the IBM/APL Scientific Centre, and released as an experimental time-sharing service for internal IBM use (at the IBM Watson Research Centre) in the autumn of 1966. It was not until 1968 that APL/360 was first released for public use.

Proponents of APL proclaim it as a consistent, concise and very powerful programming language. Much of its power is vested in the rich set of operators available, enabling easy manipulation of matrices and arrays of highest rank.

APL programs are capable of handling text as well as numerics. It has been used in most fields of programming, but less obvious uses include text editing, system simulation and teaching. The APL user utilizes the system from a terminal device in a *conversational* manner.

LOGO

Another language which comes into this classification and which is available on a number of personal computers is LOGO. It was developed as part of an experiment for teaching very small children. It is mainly known for its 'turtle graphics'.

REAL-TIME LANGUAGES

CORAL 66, derived from ALGOL 60, RTL/2, loosely based on ALGOL 68 and MODULA-2, from the PASCAL stable are all examples of real-time languages, although it is possible to quibble about the exactness of this classification. However, of all such languages, the one which stands out the most is *Ada*. The name comes from Lady Augusta Ada, Countess Lovelace, daughter of Lord Byron. She is reputed to be the first programmer. As a language, ADA was developed by the American Defense department and is mandatory for mission critical applications. The UK is also expected to adopt ADA for such work. ADA proves to be a rich and complex language.

SYSTEMS LANGUAGES

At one time, all operating system programming was done in assembly code. There are now a number of high level languages for this kind of work. They combine the control and data structures of the high level but also include facilities for manipulating binary patterns and for absolute addressing.

C was originally developed as an implementation tool for the UNIX operating system. Since compilers of C exist on a range of machines, programs written in C are highly portable.

3
Decision Tables

Decision tables have been in existence for a number of years. The era of initial development took place in the late 1950s when General Electric of the United States made the first significant use of such tables. The idea of using a table to lay out or formalize information is not new, e.g. train/airport arrival–departure tables, cricket score boards (tables), are part of everyday life.

Decision tables in computer usage have the same aim of trying to display information clearly and at a glance; but the information is restricted to 'what actions to take as a result of some decision'. In other words, certain conditions are specified in tabular format as well as the resulting actions.

EXAMPLE 1: SERVICING A CAR

Let us take a simple example of servicing a car. We might ask 'Is petrol low?' 'Is oil low?'. These two conditions lead to four possible combinations:

- both petrol and oil are low;
- only petrol is low;
- only oil is low;
- neither is low.

Each of the above will result in a different activity:

- get petrol and oil;
- get petrol only;

- get oil only;
- get neither.

In table form, this can be set out as shown in figure A3.1, where each column shows the actions to be taken as the result of a different combination of conditions. A little jargon is now necessary – but it is quite simple and painless. The table is divided into two horizontal and two vertical bands resulting in four distinct areas or quadrants.

CONDITIONS		RULES			
		2	3	4	
1.	IS PETROL LOW	Y	Y	N	N
2.	IS OIL LOW	Y	N	Y	N
ACTIONS					
1.	GET PETROL	X	X		
2.	GET OIL	X		X	
3.	GET NEITHER				X

Figure A3.1

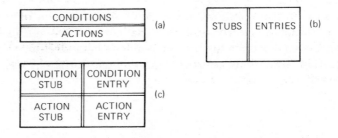

Figure A3.2

The quadrants are usually separated by double or thick black lines. If the stub (sometimes called statement/logic/parameter) portion completely defines the condition (or action), it is called a *limited entry*, since the entry sections are not required to complete the condition stub or the action stub. Figure A3.1 shows examples of limited entries in both condition and action stub. If the stub portion does not completely express the condition (or action) then it is called an *extended entry*. In these cases, the entries must contain more information than merely YES, NO or X to indicate action.

The final piece of jargon to contend with is the *rule*; this consists of a set of both conditions and resulting actions where one rule corresponds to one vertical column in the entry section. For example, in figure A3.1, rule 2 states 'if petrol is low (i.e. Y = YES) and oil is not low (N = NO)', then the action to take is 'get petrol only (denoted by an X)'.

EXAMPLE 2: MAIL ORDERING

Let us now take another example and suppose that we have a mail ordering firm sending out literature to various groups of people. These groups are:

group 1 – females between 25 and 60
group 2 – females under 25
group 3 – males under 60
group 4 – males and females 60 and over

If our firm has computerized its mailing system, then a program will exist which will 'look at' the sex and age of a given individual and place him/her in one of the groups. Forgetting about decision tables for the moment, let us attempt to construct that part of the program plan which will identify the group an individual will be classed in. Rather than use flowcharts, we shall use the simpler 'tree-chart' method. Various charts could be drawn, the one we demonstrate favours finding G4 and G3 more quickly since it 'recognizes' an individual in one of these groups more quickly than a G1 or G2 individual.

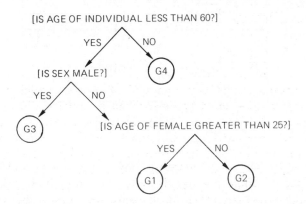

Note that the tree-chart merely describes in a two-dimensional way the necessary program logic (conditions, decisions) to arrive at any one of the four groups. This is all a decision table will show – just the logic –

but in a more direct manner. Figure A3.3 shows the decision table and it is useful to point out that the order of the conditions is not important. Any order could be used whereas with the tree-chart many different charts would be drawn each one arriving at a particular group first.

The dashes (—) used in the columns under the rule heading indicate that the corresponding conditions are irrelevant. Note that the action is an extended entry since the complete action to be taken can only be fully stated by looking (extending one's search) into the action entry quadrant.

CONDITION NUMBER	CONDITIONS	RULE NUMBER				
		1	2	3	4	
1	AGE less than 60	Y	—	Y	N	Limited entries
2	AGE greater than 25	Y	N	—	—	
3	SEX IS MALE	N	N	Y	—	
ACTION NUMBER	ACTION	ACTION NUMBER				
		1	2	3	4	Extended entry
1	CLASSIFY AS GROUP	G1	G2	G3	G4	

Figure A3.3

Had dashes not been used, how many rules would we have ended up with? There is a simple way to find out. If c stands for the number of conditions, then 2^c will be the number of rules. In our case $c = 3$, thus, $2^3 = 8$ is the correct number of rules. Figure A3.4 shows all eight rules.

	CONDITIONS	RULES							
		1	2	3	4	5	6	7	8
1	AGE less than 60	Y	Y	Y	Y	N	N	N	N
2	AGE greater than 25	Y	Y	N	N	Y	N	Y	N
3	SEX IS MALE	Y	N	N	Y	Y	Y	N	N
	CLASSIFY AS GROUP.....	G3	G1	G2	G3	G4	?	G4	?

Figure A3.4

However, certain rules can be combined, e.g. rules 1 and 4 both lead to a G3 result, therefore one is redundant and both rules may be combined. It can be seen that the answer to condition 2 (age greater than 25) is irrelevant and can be replaced with a dash. The same technique can be applied to rules 5 and 7. Both lead to a G4 indicating that the answer to condition 3 is irrelevant and may be replaced with a dash and the two rules combined (see figure A3.5). It can also happen because of

CONDITIONS		RULES							
		1	4		R3	5	7		R4
1	AGE less than 60	Y	Y		Y	N	N		N
2	AGE greater than 25	Y	N	becomes	–	Y	Y	becomes	Y
3	SEX IS MALE	Y	Y		Y	Y	N		–
ACTION	CLASSIFY AS GROUP......	G3	G3		G3	G4	G4		G4

Figure A3.5

a certain relationship between some conditions that an apparent ambiguity or impossible situation arises. If we look more closely at rules 6 and 8 it is not possible for either of these rules to occur because the answer to conditions 1 and 2 cannot both be NO at the same time. Therefore, by combining rules 1 and 4, 5 and 7 and removing rules 6 and 8 the number of rules can be reduced from eight to four as we had in figure A3.3.

A little more study will reveal that only one answer is really necessary to arrive at a G4, viz, a negative reply to condition 1 (AGE *less* than 60). It is sheer redundancy to ask for an answer to condition 2. This can also be seen for rule 2 of figure A3.3, hence the redundancy of condition 1.

It is clear that decision tables do not describe the total program but only that part which involves the logic/decisions/conditions of a certain section of the program. Since this logic information is captured in tabular form, it is easier to read than an equivalent flowchart or tree chart which in addition to the logic must also show the sequence in which individual decisions are taken in order to arrive at the actions. In this sense decision tables contain *less* information. Consequently, decision tables are not seen as an alternative to flowcharts or tree charts but as a supplement or complement. They are useful to determine whether any combination of conditions have been omitted, this is less easy to achieve with a flowchart.

CONCLUSIONS

Decision tables provide a useful documentary aid between the systems analyst and the programmer. Thus, the programmer responsible for the total plan of the eventual program may include a symbol at a given point in his flowchart indicating that the actual decision table will have to be 'consulted' at that point in order that the conditions may be processed and the resulting action determined. After the 'consultation', the program plan continues in the usual way – figure A3.6 illustrates.

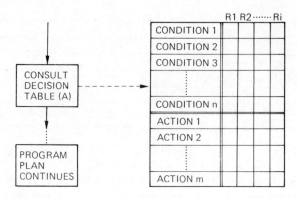

Figure A3.6

At an early stage in the development of decision tables and high-level languages, it was recognized that the decision table could be converted into program instructions. The first table translators emerged in 1965 but due to their limited ability were little used. Much improved 'second generation' translators became available from 1970 and are now more widely used for many high-level languages such as COBOL, FORTRAN and RPG.

Decision tables have not been examined in great detail since their use implies practical involvement with a computing project. The examples provided here are of a trivial nature and in practice would not warrant the use of a decision table. Clearly, they are of most value when the conditions are numerous as, say, in deciding a premium rating for a life insurance policy. Current translators are capable of accepting not only limited entries (a limitation of the first generation) but also, extended entries; they can produce program instructions equivalent to the best 'hand coded' versions that human programmers achieve; and can also check for completeness, lack of redundancy and ambiguity.

Glossary

accumulator   part of the ALU consisting of a special register and associated circuitry to perform arithmetic and to store the result.

algorithm   a sequence of statements or rules defining the solution of a problem.

alphanumeric character set   the set of characters which include the alphabet and the digits 0–9. It is sometimes also taken to include all the other printing characters usually found on a typewriter.

analog   the use of a system in which the data is of a continuously variable physical quantity such as a voltage or angular position.

application   a business or other operation that is performed by a computer or with the aid of a computer – payroll, invoicing, airline reservations.

assembler   part of the system software which converts a program written in mnemonics (assembly language) into the machine code which the computer can recognize.

binary   the number system using base two and the digits one and zero.

bit   (contraction of *b*inary dig*it*) the digits one and zero used in the binary number system.

bridge   a device which connects two local area networks of a similar type.

byte   a fixed number of bits (typically 6 or 8), often corresponding to a single character.

Cambridge ring   a ring type network developed at Cambridge University and now supported by a range of manufacturers.

cartridge tape drive   a device which reads information from a compact magnetic tape encased in a cartridge and also places information on the tape.

Ceefax   the BBC's computer-based information service. The information is arranged in 'pages' which can be selected and displayed on the TV screen provided the set has been adapted for this purpose.

communications protocol   set of rules governing the interchange of data between different devices.

compact disk read only memory (CD-ROM)   high capacity but compact disk storage on which information is burnt by a laser such that the information

195

is permanent and can only be read. The disk is similar to that used for digital audio recording.

compiler   a complex program which converts a program written in a high-level language into the machine language which a computer can recognize.

complementation   a method of representing positive and negative numbers that is used to perform subtraction by addition.

computer input microfilm   microfilm with information on it which can be input to a computer system, typically to disk for subsequent use.

computer output microfilm   information stored on the computer converted into miniature images on microfilm.

configuration   the group of interconnected devices which constitutes the particular computer system.

conversational language   a terminal-oriented programming language which allows the user of the terminal to converse with the computer's software – i.e. the language translator and operating system – whilst developing and/or executing a program.

critical path analysis   a technique used in commerce and industry to plan, control and schedule major projects.

cursor   the marker that indicates the place on the VDU screen where the next character to be entered will be displayed. Typically the marker flashes on and off to draw attention to the position.

data   information coded and structured for subsequent processing, generally, by a computer system.

data processing   the processing of information, specifically business type information, by computer.

digital   the use of binary digits to represent, store or manipulate data.

drum plotter   a graphics plotting device which plots on paper fixed to a drum that rotates backwards and forwards to accommodate the print position.

electronic mail   the transfer of messages between computer users over networks; typically a message is retained on a disk until the recipient is ready to read it.

electronic office   an office which operates using information represented in electronic form; conceptionally the office is paperless.

erasable compact disk   a high capacity compact disk on which stored information can be erased and replaced (this type of disk is at the development stage).

erasable PROM (EPROM)   similar to PROM except that the program may be erased by a special device and re-programmed many times.

Ethernet   a local-area network developed by Intel, Xerox and Digital Equipment Co, which makes use of coaxial cable.

field   a predetermined section of a record.

file   an organized collection of related records.

flatbed plotter   a graphics output device which plots on paper attached to a flat surface.

floating point notation   a form of notation in which numbers are expressed as a fractional value (mantissa) followed by an integer exponent of the base.

floppy disk   a flexible, plastic magnetic disk commonly used as backing storage for microcomputer systems.

gateway   an interface device between two networks of different type.

graphics board   (also called graphics pad and graphics tablet) a device used to input line drawings directly into the computer.

hand-held data entry terminal   a hand-held device similar in size to a calculator; the device normally has a small amount of memory and a small keyboard for data entry.

hardware   a term used to refer to the physical units which comprise a computer system.

hexadecimal   the number system with a base of 16, using the single characters, A, B, C, D, E and F as digits to represent the numbers 10, 11, 12, 13, 14 and 15 respectively.

high level language   a problem-orientated language, in that it is not machine orientated and permits the programmer to write instructions more easily according to a given class of application.

impact printer   a printing device that strikes a ribbon to deposit ink on paper.

indexed sequential access   the process of storing or retrieving data directly, but only after reading an index to locate the address of that item.

information retrieval   recovering information from stored data.

integrated circuits   circuits used in third generation computers in which the components are chemically formed on a single piece of semi-conductor material.

interface   used generally within computing to refer to a communication link between two otherwise distinct bodies – for example the I/O devices act as an interface between the internal world of the CPU and the external world of man.

K   1K = 1024. 1 byte = 8 bits and is normally the space required to store 1 character. 64K bytes therefore provides storage capacity for 64 x 1024 (65,526) characters of information.

key field   one field in a record which can be used to uniquely identify one record from all the others in a file of records.

line printer   a fast printing device that seemingly prints a complete line at a time (rather than character by character).

linear programming   a mathematical technique (not necessarily for computer programming) which produces an optimum value (or ratio of values) for a given situation involving many variables and for which there is no single solution.

list processing   concerned with the methods by which lists are processed (ordered and manipulated within central memory) according to certain relationships between the items in the list(s).

local area network (LAN)   a communications link shared by one or more computers, terminals and, typically, various peripheral devices, and normally situated within a single premises.

location   an area of computer store identifiable by its own address in which a unit of information can be placed.

low level language a machine-orientated language in which each instruction corresponds to one machine instruction. LLLs usually fall into one of two main categories: assembly level language or machine code language.

machine code the set of instructions for a particular computer. Any program must be converted into the machine code level before the computer can run the program.

magnetic ink character recognition (MICR) recognition of stylized characters that are precisely formed and printed in magnetic ink.

Mailbox an electronic mail service that enables subscribers to send messages to each other routed through the Telecom Gold computer system. Each subscriber rents a mailbox (block of storage).

mark sense reading a method of detecting (reading) marks, typically made with a pencil (graphite marks) in predetermined positions on specially prepared forms or cards.

master file a file of data which is the principal source of information for a particular application.

matrix used in mathematics to refer to a collection of items arranged in rows and columns, such that to obtain an item, both the row number and the column number have to be identified. The frame for noughts and crosses is a square matrix of three rows by three columns.

megabyte one million bytes.

microfiche a rectangle of film on which a number of frames are recorded in rows. The two standard fiche sizes (4 x 6 inches and 3 x 5 inches) record 60 and 30 frames respectively.

microsecond one millionth of a second.

millisecond one thousandth of a second.

mini floppy disk name sometimes given to the 5¼ inch size flexible, plastic magnetic disk.

mini-packet a small block of data consistent with the size requirement of a packet switching communications system, e.g. a ring network such as the Cambridge Ring.

modem (*mo*dulator/*dem*odulator) a device to allow the conversion of bits into analog electrical impulses for transmission over telephone-type circuits, and conversion back again.

mouse an input tool used in conjunction with a monitor or display screen to control the movement and position of the cursor on the screen. This is achieved by moving the box-like mouse around a flat surface.

multiplexing transmitting two or more data streams over a single communications channel.

nanosecond one thousand-millionth of a second.

network topology the shape or design of a local area network, e.g. a ring network (ring shaped).

non-impact printers an output device that prints characters or lines of characters without employing a hammer-like (typewriter) action, e.g. a thermal printer or laser printer.

object code the machine code equivalent of the source code.

octal   the number system with a base of 8, using only the digits 0, 1, 2, 3, 4, 5, 6 and 7.

office automation   the application of technology, specifically computers, to office practice (tasks).

off-line spooling   the process of transferring information to or from a secondary storage device under the direction of a satellite computer, thus allowing the main CPU to perform other tasks.

operating system   a major part of the system software which essentially supervises the running of users' programs.

operational (operations) research (OR)   the application of scientific procedures to decision making.

optical character recognition (OCR)   recognition of stylized characters that are precisely formed using light sensing methods.

optical mark reading (OMR)   a method of detecting (reading) marks made with a pen, biro or pencil in predetermined positions on specially prepared forms or cards using light sensing methods.

Oracle   the IBAs computer-based information service. The information is arranged in 'pages' (equivalent to a screen display) which can be selected and displayed on the TV screen provided the set has been adapted for the purpose.

packages   programs written for general use in a specified application.

packet   a block of information of a set size complete with address and routing instructions for tranfer over a network.

packet switching   the principal method of operation for the transfer of data over communications networks.

packet switching exchange (PSE)   a facility that checks, routes and transmits packets over a network in addition to interfacing with users of the network.

page printer   printers that operate so fast that they appear to produce a whole page of output at a time, e.g. a laser printer.

peripheral devices   the input, output and storage devices normally operated under computer control.

pixels   (contraction of picture elements) the smallest element of a display.

Prestel   British Telecom's version of Viewdata which is based on the telephone as well as the television. A Viewdata system allows two-way transmission of data, i.e. a user can interact with the information data base (for a fee).

primary storage   the main store (or memory) of the CPU – also known as main or central memory and immediate access store.

program   a set of instructions which a computer can recognize and which has been ordered in a logical sequence of steps to complete a particular task.

programmable function key   one of a set of special keys on a terminal keyboard (intelligent device) which carries out a specific function or task on the single depression of the key. The function can be determined and set up (pre-programmed) by the user, hence the name.

programmable ROM (PROM)   a type of ROM on which a program may be written after manufacture, perhaps by the purchaser. From then on, it acts as a ROM.

random access memory (RAM)   memory, usually on a chip, which can be read from and written to by the programmer. For this reason it is also known as read/write memory.

read only memory (ROM)   memory which cannot be written to, but is only read from. The software in the chip is fixed during manufacture.

real-time   a system that is able to receive continuously changing data from outside sources and to process that data sufficiently quickly to be capable of influencing the sources of data (e.g. air traffic control).

record   a collection of related items of data, treated as a single unit for processing.

register   a special location in the CPU which has a specific purpose, e.g. an accumulator that accumulates results as a program is executed. Typically a computer has a set of registers for different purposes.

scanner   an input device that reads printed text employing optical character recognition techniques (pattern matching).

secondary storage   an area of storage separate from the main memory of a computer – synonymous with backing storage and auxiliary storage.

semi-conductors   used to form small compact circuitry which can also be used to form memory.

serial printer   a printing (output) device that prints one character at a time, e.g. a daisywheel printer.

simulation   the representation of a real situation in a computer by means of a model so that different conditions can be tested.

single chip microcomputer   a microcomputer with the control unit, arithmetic unit, and memory all on the one chip.

software   a collection of programs written to bring the hardware of a computer system into operation and to best advantage.

source code   the program written in the language chosen by the programmer, such as FORTRAN or PASCAL.

string   a sequence of one or more characters.

systems analysis   the task of determining how best to implement a user's application on a particular computer system. The process involves analysing the existing system; determining the feasibility of the conversion; producing the design and then testing the final conversion.

teletext   a system for broadcasting text in conjunction with broadcast television, e.g Ceefax (BBC) and Oracle (IBA).

time sharing   a means of providing multi-access to a computer system. Each user is allowed a time-slice of the system's resources, although each appears to have continuous use of the system.

token ring   a ring-shaped network which operates on the principle that a node or station on the ring is only able to take on board and transmit data when in possession of a so-called 'token'.

touch-sensitive screen   a terminal that acts on the touch (fingertip) of the screen rather than through keyed input. The action that occurs depends on which point of the screen is touched in relation to the software (program) in use at the time.

transaction file   a collection of records treated as a file which is used to update a master file.

transceiver   literally a device that can both transmit and receive. Each device requiring connection to an Ethernet is joined through a transceiver.

transistor   a small, light, very fast switching device within the electronics of second generation computers. (Also used in amplifiers.)

Viewdata   a computer-based information system accessed via a telephone which can provide a display of the selected information on an adapted TV screen. Any page on the database can be called but no page is transmitted unless selected.

wide area network (WAN)   a network spanning a sizeable geographical area with communication based on the telephone system, satellites or microwave transmission.

word   a collection of bits treated as a single unit.

work station   an intelligent terminal or microcomputer equipped with sufficient storage space and appropriate output device to enable specific work to be carried out at the station (locally). Typically, the work station will be connected to one or more computers and other peripheral equipment via a network to supplement the application or for different applications.

write once, read memory (WORM)   optical disk memory which can be written on once only and thereafter only read.

Acronyms

ALGOL	algorithm language
ALU	arithmetic/logic unit
APL	a programming language
APT	automatically programmed tools
BASIC	beginners' all purpose symbolic instruction code
CAD	computer-aided design
CAE	computer-aided engineering
CAI	computer-aided instruction
CAL	computer-aided learning
CIM	computer input microfilm
COBOL	common business oriented language
COM	computer output (originated) microfilm
CP	central processor
CPU	central processing unit
CRT	cathode ray tube
CU	control unit
EDSAC	electronic delay storage automatic calculator
EDVAC	electronic discrete variable automatic calculator
ENIAC	electronic numeric integrator and calculator
EPROM	erasable programmable read only memory
FORTRAN	formula translator
HIPO	hierarchical input/process/output
IAS	Institute for Advanced Study
IBM	International Business Machines
ICL	International Computers Limited
JANET	Joint Academic Network
LAN	local area network

LCD	liquid crystal display
LEO	Lyons Electronic Office
LISP	list processing
LSI	large scale integration
MICR	magnetic ink character recognition
MPU	micro-processor unit
MSI	medium scale integration
NCR	National Cash Registers
OCR	optical character recognition
OMR	optical mark recognition
PL/1	Programming Language 1
PROM	programmable read only memory
PSE	packet switching exchange
PSS	packet switched system
RAM	random access memory
ROM	read only memory
RPG	report program generator
RTL	real time language
SEAC	Standards Eastern Automatic Computer
SEAQ	Stock Exchange Automated Quotations
SIMULA	simulation language – an extension of ALGOL for simulation language problems
SNOBOL	string oriented symbolic language
SSADM	structured systems analysis and design methodology
SSI	small scale integration
UNIVAC	universal automatic computer
VDU	visual display unit
WAN	wide area network
WORM	write once, read memory

References

Auerbach, I. L.: 'The impact of information processing on mankind.' In Popplewell (ed.) *Information Processing* Rotterdam, North Holland Publishing Company, 1962.

Bohm, C. and Jacopini, C.: 'Flow diagrams, Turing Machines and languages with only two format rules.' *Communications of the ACM,* **9**, 5, 1962.

British Computer Society Glossary Working Party (eds): *A Glossary of Computing Terms: An Introduction* (5th edition) Cambridge University Press, 1985.

Dijkstra, E. W.: 'Goto statement considered harmful'. Letter to *Communications of the ACM* **11**, 3, 1968.

Galland, F. J.: *Dictionary of Computing* Chichester, John Wiley and Sons, 1979.

Randell, B. (ed): *The Origins of Digital Computers – Selected Papers* Berlin, Springer Verlag, 1973.

Schneider, G.M. *et al.*: *An Introduction to Programming and Problem Solving with Pascal* (2nd edition) New York, John Wiley and Sons, 1982.

Index

range guns on ships and tanks meant that armies had to fight by shooting at targets they could not see. Technology, in the form of radar, was developed to locate the enemy: where he was, in which direction he was moving and how fast he was travelling. It was then necessary to aim guns so that when the shell was fired it would reach the enemy at the point to which he had moved. This could not be done with any accuracy without first performing detailed mathematical calculations. Firing tables were required by the men at the front line so that the figures were immediately available. But these figures were not in existence because the human effort involved in producing them was too great. What was needed was a machine which could produce the tables with the required speed and accuracy. Huge sums of money and brainpower were combined to produce the technology. In 1942, the Ballistic Research Laboratory of the US Army Ordnance Department began work with the Moore School of Electrical Engineering. As a result, a computer named ENIAC had a formal dedication ceremony on 15 February, 1946 (see Appendix One). ENIAC was able to produce the tables by carrying out the huge number of calculations involved, accurately and to the required precision and, because it was electronic, at a speed which made it all possible.

The problems which early computers had to solve were mostly mathematical. Today, computers are used to forecast the weather, to operate machines to cut shapes out of sheet metal, and even to guide spacecraft to the moon. They can set and print newspapers and books. They can be used to help in diagnosing diseases and to find out whether a hospital bed is available for a particular patient. They are used to find obscure documents in archives and elusive criminals on the run. Travel agents around the world have come to rely on them to book seats on air flights or rooms in hotels, either today or a year from now. Companies use them for accounting, invoicing, stock control and payrolls. Computer **applications** are discussed in detail in Chapter Nine.

The original objective for inventing the computer was to create a fast calculating machine. But in over 80% of computing today, the applications are of a non-mathematical or non-numerical nature. To define a computer merely as a calculating device is to ignore over 80% of its work, rather like someone refusing to believe that the bulk of the iceberg lies hidden under the water. If not as a calculating device, then how are we to define a computer?

If we return to the brief list of applications above, we can discern one key fact: computers act upon information. This information or **data,** comes in all shapes and sizes, from a mathematical equation to the required details about a company's work-force necessary to produce a payroll, or to the myriad of data needed to project an Apollo craft

1

An Introduction to Computing

WHY WAS THE COMPUTER INVENTED?

`Many of the routine activities in today's society are performed by computers. For example, when we go on holiday our 'plane seats are often reserved by computers; the traffic in some major cities is, to a degree, controlled by computers; the egg which you might have had for breakfast may have been laid (no, not by a computer!) by a chicken whose life history is on record on a computer file; many of the bills we pay (rates, gas, electricity, telephone, insurance, etc.) are calculated and printed by a computer. Why? And how?

It was outlined in the Introduction that there are three essential concepts that we need to examine in order to be able to think sensibly and talk intelligently about computing – What are computers? What can they do? How can we communicate with them? But first of all, what do the terms *computer* and *computing* mean?

Obviously computing has something to do with reckoning or calculation, but man has been using his brain to do just that for centuries. The Egyptians built the pyramids; whoever built Stonehenge left a calendar which can still accurately predict eclipses; the Romans designed and built long straight roads, aqueducts and heating systems; early explorers navigated the globe, and even radio and television were invented – all without computers. What is so special about them that we need computers today? It cannot simply be because they are calculating devices. We have many forms of such devices – the abacus (still used in the Far East), pocket and desk calculators, even supermarket check-out tills – all of which are cheaper and easier to use than computers. So, why was the computer invented?

Because it had to be! The pressures of World War !I dictated research in many areas. The new use of night bombers, submarines, and long

1

through space. The fact that computers process information is so fundamental, some experts have coined a word for it – *informatics*, the science of information processing, i.e., the methods of recording, manipulating and retrieving information. Many people believe this to be the essence of computing.

THE MACHINE

Before the days of electrical engineering, attempts had been made to provide results to mathematical problems by *mechanical* means. In the early nineteenth century, Charles Babbage came closest to succeeding. At that time, mathematical and statistical tables (for insurance companies and government records, for example) had to be compiled by small armies of clerks. Working as they did, without the help of adding machines, even the most elaborate precautions could not eliminate human errors. Babbage spent many tedious hours checking tables. From his dissatisfaction and, probably, exasperation with the clerks' inaccuracies, came the idea of a machine which could compute tables guaranteed to be error-free. Among many other achievements, Babbage designed several 'engines' as he called them, the first of these being the Difference Engine. This was built in 1822 and produced the first reliable life tables (statistics of expectation of life) which were in use for the next 50 years.

In 1833, Babbage began work on his Analytical Engine and it is this machine with which we are concerned. His requirements for precision engineering were impossible to achieve at that time and, therefore, he was unable to produce a working model of the complete, and massive, machine. Had he done so, it would have been the forerunner of today's electronic computer. But notes and drawings describe what he had in mind. The Analytical Engine was intended to be completely automatic. It was to be capable of performing the basic arithmetical functions for *any* mathematical problem and it was to do so at a speed of 60 additions a minute. The machine was to consist of five parts:

- a *store* in which to hold numbers, i.e., those which were to provide the information (data) for the problems, and those which were to be generated during the course of calculations
- an *arithmetic unit* which Babbage called the 'mill'. This was to be a device for performing the arithmetical operations on the numbers which had been stored. All the operations were to have been carried out automatically through rotations of gears and wheels
- a *control unit* for seeing that the machine performed the desired operations in the correct sequence and, also by means of a series

of gears and wheels, for transferring data between the mill and the store

– and *input device* to pass into the machine both numbers (the data) and instructions as to which of the arithmetical operations to perform

– an *output device* to display the results obtained from the calculations.

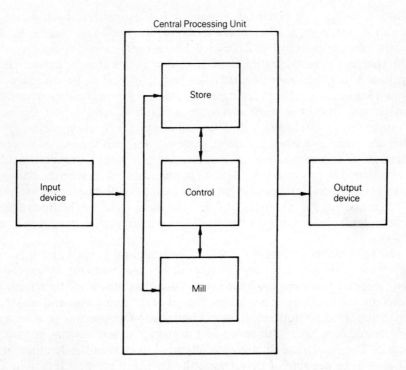

Figure 1.1

Figure 1.1 shows these five parts in an arrangement which closely resembles the basic anatomy of today's computer. The three parts consisting of the Store, Mill and Control units are collectively known, in current terminology, as the Central Processing Unit (CPU) (discussed in greater detail in the next chapter). It is this to which we really refer when talking about the computer. The other two units, the Input and Output devices (I/O) (see Chapter Four), are concerned with entering information (instructions and data) into the CPU, and with outputting the results once processing has taken place.